Kyle Powell is a born and raised Londoner, whose passion for writing began at a young age. Kyle enjoys writing about philosophy, love, justice, and life from both non-fiction and fiction angles. Kyle is keen to write about issues that impact the Black community, particularly from the perspective of the Diaspora.

Kyle has spent time working as a mentor with secondary school students, before becoming project leader. During his time as a mentor, he worked to help increase leadership qualities and lateral thinking for students from disadvantaged backgrounds. He also has worked in and led Diversity and Inclusion (D&I) teams at two large pharmaceutical companies. Kyle's work in the healthcare D&I space included addressing under-representation in clinical trials, increasing psychological safety, and improving knowledge and understanding around racial disparities and experiences.

Kyle has a BSc and MSc in Neuroscience from the University of Bristol and King's College London. Following his academic studies developing his scientific and critical thinking skills, Kyle reconnected with his love of writing as part of his career in the healthcare industry as a communications consultant and subsequently a commercial director.

Kyle is a lifelong Arsenal fan and loves to listen to music, play football, and travel, whenever he is not writing.

To all of those who came before; power and purpose to all of those who come after.

The goal is to pass the baton in varying increments of progression contributing to a common goal.

Kyle Powell

THE DIASPORA DILEMMA

AUSTIN MACAULEY PUBLISHERS™
LONDON • CAMBRIDGE • NEW YORK • SHARJAH

Copyright © Kyle Powell 2023

The right of Kyle Powell to be identified as author of this work has been asserted by the author in accordance with sections 77 and 78 of the Copyright, Designs and Patents Act 1988.

All rights reserved. No part of this publication may be reproduced, stored in a retrieval system, or transmitted in any form or by any means, electronic, mechanical, photocopying, recording, or otherwise, without the prior permission of the publishers.

Any person who commits any unauthorised act in relation to this publication may be liable to criminal prosecution and civil claims for damages.

The story, the experiences, and the words are the author's alone.

A CIP catalogue record for this title is available from the British Library.

ISBN 9781398482241 (Paperback)
ISBN 9781398482258 (ePub e-book)

www.austinmacauley.com

First Published 2023
Austin Macauley Publishers Ltd®
1 Canada Square
Canary Wharf
London
E14 5AA

This book was a long time in the making; the inspiration and support of many people have helped me to complete it. As always, I have to thank my mum, sister and family for providing me with a loving foundation and constant support. I would also like to thank all of the inspiring authors who helped me on my own journey: Frantz Fanon, James Baldwin, Angela Davis, Harriet A. Washington, Michelle Alexander, Mehrsa Baradaran, to name a few.

From a more foundational view, I would like to thank some inspirational figures that helped shape my journey of knowledge and justice: Marcus Garvey, Steven Biko, Malcolm X, again, just to name a few.

Table of Contents

Preface	11
Chapter 1: Introduction	16
Chapter 2: Level Setting: A Historical Overview	25
Chapter 3: Economic Anchors	35
Chapter 4: The Impact of Economics – Socio-Economics	64
Chapter 5: Society	76
Chapter 6: Law, Government and Politics	114
Chapter 7: Narratives, Media, Music and Entertainment	153
Chapter 8: Sports, Sports and the Plantation	190
Chapter 9: Psychological and Mental Health	209
Chapter 10: In Closing	239
Epilogue	247
Recommended Reading	249
References	251

Preface

We're all on a journey. Here's how mine led to this book...

I'm an '80s' baby, born and raised in North London in an area called Tottenham. Tottenham became home to many people of Caribbean and African heritage who had migrated to the UK in search of a better life. It seems a bit of a cliché to say that I was born in a time of turmoil, but in many ways, I was. The infamous riots that took place in one of Tottenham's largest estates, Broadwater Farm, took place the year before I was born. The backlash was triggered by four policemen breaking into the home of Cynthia Jarrett in search of stolen property (which incidentally was never found). The aggressive intrusion caused Cynthia to die of heart failure.[1] Of course, the unrest was not triggered by this one isolated incident but rather it was the straw that broke the camel's back, following years of tension between the Black community and the police. This is something we sadly still see decades later, perhaps most notably in 2011 with the police killing of unarmed Mark Duggan and the subsequent riots across the UK.[2]

Throughout my life, I have experienced milestone moments that have awakened me to the inequities and injustice faced by the African Diaspora in the West, the first of which occurred when I was relatively young. I was fortunate enough to do the majority of my growing up in a 'nicer' part of the city; my mum managed to move us to an area with low crime and good schools. While my upbringing was working class, I was very much surrounded by the middle classes, which offered a perspective into a different way of living. What I learnt most from where I grew up came from the contrast experienced by the majority of my family who remained in Tottenham and similar areas: the contrast between reality and opportunity. I could see the difference in schooling I received compared to family members who lived in different parts of the city. I could see the subconscious mental engineering that we all encounter, what some would term being a 'product of your environment'. A very real concept that works both ways, not just for those who grow up in 'difficult' spaces but also for those who are afforded privilege and opportunity. The seeds of disparity were being sown in my mind.

In 1993, Steven Lawrence was killed in a racially motivated attack.[3] I was seven years old. The police inquest was shambolic and uncovered institutional racism throughout the London Metropolitan Police Force. Ironically, it was around the time of his death that I discovered my passion for writing—nothing polished, of course, simply enjoyment for the activity just as I fell in love with football around the same time.

My first truly revolutionary spark came when I was 14; I was in a Personal and Social Education (PSE) class watching a film about Steven Biko, the anti-apartheid activist. His struggle for the liberation of Black South Africans and his martyrdom were inspirational. Not long after, I was given a copy of Malcolm X's autobiography. The journey of smart-talking street hustler 'Red', or Malcolm Little, to one of the leading lights in the Civil Rights movement, was spellbinding to me, even at a time when racial injustice was largely suppressed by mainstream media and before the advent of one of the world's most powerful communications tools, social media.

During my secondary school years, university education, and the beginning of work life, I would often come across what we would now term microaggressions with a smattering of overt direct racism, but in a pre-social-media world, there wasn't the exposure or attention to really shine a light on the struggle people in the Diaspora were facing. I was fortunate enough to have an element of protection because of my education and career. While being the only Black face in the lecture theatre or office was normal, the challenges facing my community were not invisible to me.

The shooting of Mark Duggan in 2011 was another watershed moment for me. At the time, I was living in a flat-share in Wood Green with two friends, providing ringside seats to the unrest. We didn't have to watch the news; we could literally look out the window. In the aftermath, the political discourse and deconstruction of the events by mainly middle-aged White men on BBC's *Newsnight* and other such shows were clearly missing the frustration of the masses. This was not just about the police oppression of Black people; it was a much broader outcry of disenfranchisement, of being left behind—millions of people who felt they had little to no stake in society, many of whom were Black. This was a wake-up call for me. It made me question what was going on: made me question the inequity and injustice faced by those in the working class—those who in London largely looked like me. Slowly, the penny was starting to drop—the connection between race, oppression, housing, opportunity… Suddenly, the stories of past revolutionaries didn't seem so distant. When we think of Malcolm X, Marcus Garvey, and Mandela, there is a tendency to think that these are soldiers from an old war, a fight that is over as we are now in a 'post-racial peace time'. Slowly but surely that myth was being untangled.

I decided to get involved with mentoring. I've always admired teachers; their ability to positively impact the lives of children in their formative years is a real gift. Everyone remembers their good teachers, the ones that helped them, gave them confidence, even inspired them. Mentoring was a way I could have a similar impact while keeping my day job. Giving back, helping kids from less privileged backgrounds, provided me more satisfaction than any job I've ever had; it was a truly special experience. A lot of what the mentoring programme was about was giving these kids experiences they would not normally get, a chance to see worlds that are usually shut off to those from lower-income families. We would take them to different companies and let them see first-hand what they could do if they applied themselves. Seeing things for yourself can be very inspirational; and seeing people that look like you in these roles, even more so. Taking the kids to my office was a great experience, and I thoroughly enjoyed all the work I did as a mentor. However, it also gave me another opportunity to see the disparities that are present in different communities, particularly those in the Diaspora.

Fast-forward to 2014, across the pond, Obama was established in office and preparing for a second term, his message of hope and change bringing positivity to millions around the world. Depending on your experience, broadly things did not seem so bad, or at least no worse than they ever were. This, for me at least, was about to change. Eric Garner, Tamir Rice and Michael Brown were all killed by the police in 2014.[4] Moreover, there was video evidence of the events, evidence that was shown around the world, evidence that was a stark reminder of what it meant to be Black in the West. For me and many others who had the privilege (despite our own problems with the police) of living in a society where the police don't carry guns, these were shocking scenes. These camera phone state-sponsored murders kicked my reading into overdrive. It was clear that we had not moved past issues of race despite having a Black president; in reality, it didn't mean anything.

The more I read, the more I learned, the clearer the picture became—the cross-sectional barriers and injustices that were set up for people in the Diaspora. It took me a while to fully piece things together. When I did, I wanted to share what I'd discovered and help people get this information in an easier way than I did and sooner. When writing, I often think I want to write stuff that I wish someone else had written, something I would want to read. I tried to manifest that desire with this book: something that will serve people, providing greater clarity and depth of understanding of the challenges and potential solutions to the dilemmas facing the African Diaspora in the West. Now you have my journey; time to get into the book.

Chapter 1: Introduction

'Liberate the minds of men and ultimately you will liberate the bodies of men.'[5]
– Marcus Garvey

In this chapter:

- The aims and scope of the book
- The importance of being able to navigate problems
- How overcoming fear can bring us closer

The first question you probably have is, 'What is The Diaspora Dilemma?' The dilemma is the composite amalgamation of the racial challenges faced by those of African descent who now reside primarily in the West (The Diaspora). I explore those challenges and some of the ways in which these challenges could be transcended. I provide summaries for the challenges faced and paths forward for different sections of the world we live in e.g. economics, health, media, and entertainment. These are intended to provide an overview of different areas to allow the bigger picture to be seen, but in truth, each section could be a book in its own right.

There are three main things I hope to achieve in this book:

- To help all people better understand the challenges faced by the African Diaspora in the West in order to help create a more cohesive society.
- To propose potential solutions to these challenges—ways to improve the problems that are faced by the African Diaspora in the West.
- To improve the understanding and interconnected nature of the challenges facing those in the African Diaspora, with the hope of helping people from the Diaspora navigate these challenges successfully.

As the old axiom states, 'knowledge is power'.[6] I would go a step further and say understanding is power. If you understand how something works, you have the potential to change it. This book aims to help people understand the state of play for people of the African Diaspora in the Western world, the interconnected web that has created our reality, and some guidance as to how we can navigate and progress in a constructive way.

I want people to feel liberated through greater understanding, to feel inspired by some of the great things already happening and opportunities that are available. Yes, there are many problems in the world; challenges to face and barriers to overcome, but there is a genuine chance to transcend, achieve, and succeed. I believe this can be done in a collective manner, with people from all backgrounds working together, but much of the work has to happen from within the community. From the perspective of the White community since George Floyd's death, I've lost count of the number of people who have said to me they 'didn't know' how bad things were and have been. This is both a manifestation of the privilege of not having to know and simultaneously an indictment of our education systems and society at large that has decided that this knowledge and understanding is not a priority.

W.E.B. Du Bois once said: 'And herein lies the tragedy of the age: not that men are poor—all men know something of poverty; not that men are wicked—who is good? Not that men are ignorant—what is Truth? Nay, but that men know so little of men.'[7]

It is easy to get bogged down in the difficulties that we all have to face as individuals in the twenty-first century. The narratives perpetuated by the media are usually negative ones, and the amplification of social media can sometimes make it all feel inescapable. Whether it's another case of police brutality, a disparaging comment from a world leader or an episode of 'Black-on-Black' crime (or just crime in the Black community, as would be more accurate terminology), it can feel like there is little hope or chance of progression. Greater clarity about the bigger picture can help with navigating these obstacles.

Navigation, Achievement and Progress

The challenges that face people of the African Diaspora can seem daunting and complex. How can people from the African Diaspora succeed in a world where the cards are seemingly so stacked against them? By *understanding* the game and *playing* it well. In addition, if there is also a desire from outside of the Black community for collective progression (through allyship and other forms of support), it is important that potential allies have a better understanding of how ubiquitous and interconnected the challenges of racial prejudice are.

On the surface, the plethora of challenges that make up our modern-day reality of racial discrimination appears to be a network of many seemingly disparate topics. However, closer examination tells a different story...For example, the connection between slavery, where we have centuries of free labour without the possibility of generating resources, and the poor financial health of the Diaspora today. This financial bondage not only prevented generational wealth creation and transfer that other communities benefitted from but it was also buttressed by segregation practices for the majority of the twentieth century that restricted employment and deepened the economic burden. This along with many other contributing factors translates to a present-day reality where the Black family (Black child household) has 1 cent for every dollar of a White family (White child household)[8]—a web of oppressive institutions, each robust in its own right and then compounded by other complementary pillars—from the economic, political, historical, the media—are all related and all part of one whole.

There are a lot of different factors at play which can feel overwhelming. To me, it's like a very big puzzle with many pieces, or perhaps an intricate 3D puzzle, with lots of different parts that fit together to make one cohesive picture. To see the picture clearly you need to have all of the pieces and understand how the puzzle can be put together. Once you see how everything fits together, things become less overwhelming, and a path forward becomes clearer.

Wrecking Walls and Building Bridges

The collapse of the Berlin Wall decades ago was met with joy throughout the world. Many of those behind the Eastern side of the Iron Curtain were happy to be reunited with their kin from Western Europe. The artificial separation of people based on political ideology was dismantled and, most importantly, people were brought together. As people, the social animals we are, we naturally want to be together. This sentiment could also be observed with the backlash against former President Trump's wall at the Mexican border. I believe humans are not inherently evil or hateful. Hate and discrimination are taught and learned. Experiments with young infants show happy, natural interactions prior to learning about race and colour. And yet, a telling indictment of our society is how stereotypes of good and bad, linked to race, are imprinted at a remarkably early age.

It is also important to escape the unhelpful broad-brush generalisation that *all* White people are the enemy. It's inflammatory and inaccurate; most White people are indifferent, uninformed, and inert in terms of issues of race. However, this inertia and passive ambivalence can be detrimental to people of colour, as the systems, attitudes, and policies created to oppress Black people continue unchecked and effective to this day. There is, of course, an important distinction between those with conscious malicious intent and those who are in passive, tacit agreement with systems of oppression. The latter is comparatively better but not necessarily innocent; it is what some might consider 'Nice Racism'. If we take the discussion a level up beyond race to that of humans, we see that we all have our own struggles and challenges in life. Unfortunately, our current societal model means most people are living 'pay cheque to pay cheque', too consumed with making ends meet to be genuinely invested in issues beyond their immediate world. In short, not being as passionate about what does not impact you directly is not the same as not caring at all or being racist. I think there are many examples of where we all pay less attention to things than we should, merely because they do not immediately impact our reality; the largely passive amount of attention paid to our struggling environment is a good example of this.

This small exposition is by no means intended to exonerate White people from the role they play in supporting the systems that oppress Black people but to provide a more accurate lens on the true state of play and highlight that the majority of work needs to come from within the community, not from external handouts or favours. Independent thinking and self-determination are the key.

Overcoming Fear

As humans, we tend to fear what we don't understand. People and ideas that are different or new can seem alien and threatening. I have often faced tasks that seemed daunting at first but once the challenge was understood became manageable and less intimidating. The barriers that have been built up between people function in a similar way; whether it's learned hatred and racism or systemic discrimination, these fearful notions can lead to the world becoming a frightening place.

I believe two of the biggest political milestones of the twenty-first century to date are good examples of this, the first being the Leave campaign from the Brexit referendum and the other being the Trump 2017 US election win. The Leave campaign was largely based on fear, inflating the genuine concerns of large parts of the UK; in particular, fear that there was little to no control of UK borders and that migrants from 'unsavoury' countries would flock in and overwhelm an already stretched public sector—or that hundreds of millions of pounds could be saved weekly for the beloved National Health Service (NHS),[9] which was supposedly being syphoned off by greedy bureaucrats in Brussels. A greater understanding of the actual immigration situation at that time would have helped to dispel some of these concerns. For example, the records show that immigrants contribute far more than they take from our systems and are integral to key public services like the NHS. If people understood that, in reality, the £350 million a week promised to the NHS would never, in fact, be directly routed into public spending, then perhaps people would have been less swayed by that promise. Similarly, the Remain campaign could have done more to help assuage the concerns of millions of British people who are experiencing little economic prosperity and a real strain on their local public services. A better understanding of their concerns would have led to a more compelling campaign and helped bridge the gap for these people.

As if history were repeating itself, as it so often does, not long after Brexit was a strikingly similar campaign across the pond, where the Republican Party also played on fears of immigration, propagating the idea that the US was facing an immigration crisis in the shape of criminals and murderers from their Mexican neighbours in the south. A wall was the proposed solution. Former President Trump shut down the government until he received government funding for the divisive project. Again, a better and more comprehensive understanding of the immigration situation in the US would have rendered this deeply flawed argument far less potent. The sad irony of a country built on immigration being so fearful of immigration was lost on far too many. Unfortunately, the lack of understanding of the migrant Mexican population enabled the campaign to dehumanise them and turn them into a perceived threat to national security. Conversely, people who actually knew, interacted and understood Mexican people were much less likely to be won over by an argument that negatively tarnished the group.

Lack of comprehension leading to the acceptance of false narratives, discrimination, fear and dehumanisation of people is at the centre of racial prejudice. Fearful stereotypes are most powerful when one group of people lack understanding of another. A greater comprehension of the reality of a group can lead to greater compassion, something that is also key to building a better world. This lack of understanding can also be seen as the root of racial discrimination. I have had conversations with White people who have asked why there are so many gangs in Black or minority neighbourhoods and why do most Black people tend to live in poorer housing. This type of information is not communicated or discussed; it is just taken to be the status quo. It's what we see in the media, and there is no clear explanation for it; it just seems to be the case. This book aims to help improve the understanding of these topics with the aim of building bridges.

The Scope

The scope of the book is the people of the African Diaspora who have spread to the United States and the United Kingdom. Of course, there are people of the African Diaspora who live in many other parts of the world, from Europe to South America (e.g. Brazil and Colombia) and Asia, and many of the challenges faced are similar, but to focus the discussion and maximise my own experience and knowledge, the focus will be on the UK and the US.

I will be using Black people, African Americans, Black Brits and Black Americans fairly interchangeably. The important thing to note is I am speaking of people of colour of African descent living in the West. At times, I will be referring to specific data, experiences, or examples from groups in the UK or US, although many of the challenges are similar irrespective of location.

Chapter 2: Level Setting: A Historical Overview

'A generation which ignores history has no past and no future.'[10]
– Robert Heinlein

'We are not makers of history. We are made by history.'[11]
– Martin Luther King, Jr.

In this chapter:

- A review of the legacy and lasting impact of slavery on the present-day reality of the African Diaspora

A challenge that is often levied against people who cite the racial injustice of the past like slavery or Jim Crow, or a time where lynching was rife, is that these are things of bygone eras that no longer impact the present day. 'This was decades, if not centuries, ago,' they state, 'So why are we still talking about it? You have been free for a long time now.' In response, I would say that significant periods in history should not be forgotten just because they are in the past. It is important to recognise past atrocities out of respect for those who suffered, but more importantly to learn from them to ensure we do not repeat the same mistakes. Perhaps even more importantly than acknowledging past instances of racial injustice, it is essential to accurately understand the legacy of how said acts shape and impact present-day reality—permeating practically all aspects of society today. It is a known fact that the majority of global superpowers, particularly those in the West, built their wealth from years of colonial extraction and exploitation. If the actions of the past had no impact on the present day, these countries would not be as wealthy or powerful as they are. Likewise, if the past were irrelevant, the countries in Africa, South America, and Southern Asia, which were ravaged and underdeveloped centuries ago would be on par with the West today, but this is not the case—legacy matters.

You can see the reach of this legacy in all walks of life: racist mindsets passed down through generations that lead to some people in today's world genuinely believing that Black people are 'lesser than'; a narrative of White supremacy based largely on how they were raised; or the collective economic weakness of the majority of the Diaspora because of the limitations enforced during generations of bondage e.g. it being illegal to accumulate wealth; working for free for centuries and then practically for free for years during Reconstruction as sharecroppers, where drastically unfair economic dynamics kept Black people perpetually in debt. You can see the legacy in the brutality and public executions carried out by our contemporary police forces and other White supremacists, no different from what was taking place in what some would like to believe to be the 'distant past'.

In a similar vein, the argument that today's citizens should not be blamed for the actions of their forefathers is also often purported. This point has more credibility, of course, but it doesn't escape the legacy issue. The same benefits afforded to colonial powers through slavery and colonial exploitation were translated into the privileges of many White descendants' present-day society. They may not have executed slavery, but they do benefit from the structures created from the labour; they did not loot Africa, but they do benefit from its riches today. I was not a slave, but I suffer from the legacy of discrimination.

So, our history does count for a lot today. It has shaped the world we live in today. It influences and dictates much of our current reality. It is also important to have an awareness of where we are coming from, from where we are aiming to progress, lessons we can learn and mistakes we need to avoid.

This section is not intended to be a comprehensive overview of all the past traumatic events of racism, but rather a summary of some of the more significant moments and how they feed into contemporary times.

What to Do with These People?

As mentioned in the introduction, the purpose of the book is to create a broader understanding of the state of play for people of the African Diaspora in the West to act as guidance and encourage progress moving forward. However, to know where you are going, you have to know where you have been.

The historical context of this journey is an important one as it provides the backdrop and legacy for many of today's issues. As many are aware, the majority of Black people were forcibly brought to the Americas through the transatlantic slave trade from the 1600s through to the beginning of the nineteenth century. However, following many rebellions, the rise of industrialisation and the ultimate success of the emancipation movement, the forced imprisonment of African people ended, and they were 'technically' free. In reality, freedom was a very loose interpretation of the reality of the time, for example, vagrancy laws could easily be breached by poor former enslaved people, which would quickly place them back into a life of imposed servitude, all the way to its more modern evolution, the legacy that is mass incarceration today.

The task now for the ruling powers was what to do with all these people who were brought here to serve a purpose that they could no longer forcibly carry out. This, for me, is a key question and sets the tone for many of the subsequent challenges and barriers for people of the African Diaspora. The original intention was never to have a fully integrated and equal society. While things can evolve and progress over time, a scan through the history books will show you how difficult this has been, similar to trying to move a boulder up a steep hill, with only one hand, while being held back by an anchor.

Legacy Rules Mindset – Racial Tension and Propagation of White Supremacy

A look at the American South today will give you an example of how history can continue to permeate the present. The history of the South is one of a confederation that was so fully invested in slavery that it embarked on a civil war to continue the privilege. Lynching and terror against African Americans were common in the 1800s through to the modern era[12] but were particularly pronounced in the South through the post-slavery and civil rights era. That mentality of White superiority and hate passed through the years and generations is a key reason for some of the present-day discrimination faced today. Of course, this is not a broad-brush generalisation of all White Americans in the South nor is it an attempt to absolve former Union states or coastal elites of discriminatory acts; this is a problem that is still prevalent in the United States, Europe, South America, and elsewhere around the globe.

Another clear example of the horrors of history passed on to the present comes in the shape of law enforcement. In the United States, some of the first police officers were 'slave catchers' or 'slave patrol' (small bands of men tasked with retrieving runaway enslaved people) in the Carolinas in the early 1700s.[13] Naturally, that is not the best basis for interactions between two groups of people trying to build an integrated society—the almost literal personification of 'cops' and 'robbers'. It is important to note that not all police officers are racist or that it is some kind of prerequisite to becoming a police officer. However, like a country that originally imported people for a specific purpose, who then subsequently are not interested in the liberty of these formerly enslaved people, a police force originally created to keep people in bondage is not going to easily switch to a diametrically opposite state of protecting this group of people and their freedom—despite the main purpose of most police forces being to protect and serve all in society. Since emancipation right through to the present day, there have been frequent instances of police brutality towards people of colour in the West. The overt level of force often used and the subsequent injuries and deaths that follow are part of a long-running narrative—a story that has started to become more and more public with the advent of camera phones and the sharing capabilities of social media. While the video recording of Rodney King being severely beaten by the LA Police Department may have been seen as a one-off by people outside of the African American community, the numerous cases of strong-arm and often lethal law enforcement caught on camera in the past 10 to 15 years show a very clear pattern. The ability for so many to view and share these incidents so regularly, unsurprisingly, is quite shocking for most people who are fortunate enough to not face that level of 'policing' first-hand. Just pick any one of the state-sanctioned executions caught live on camera in recent years from across the US for a very stark reminder of how much progress still needs to be made. From Freddie Gray to Sandra Bland to George Floyd, the story is a clear one.

Resources: 40 Acres and a Mule

Following the sacrifices made for hundreds of years during slavery and for the sacrifices made during the US Civil War, on January 16, 1865, Union General William Tecumseh Sherman promised freed enslaved people 40 acres and a mule to help start their life as free men and women.[14] This promise was, of course, never honoured. The ability of the US government to renege on treaties let alone promises is nothing new as the Indigenous peoples of the Americas can attest to, time after time.

The issue of note here is one of generational wealth and the ability to build resources for future generations. Not only were enslaved people unable to generate any financial resources during the centuries of free labour, but they also were not supported in doing so when they were supposedly free. You would think that after centuries of massive wealth creation and infrastructure development that the United States and Western Europe benefitted from, there would be some recognition of the contribution of Black people. Wealth, labour, and infrastructure played a very significant role in creating their respective status as superpowers at the time and for the decades following, perhaps a bit of a *Thank You* for all that hard work would not be too much to ask. Apparently, it was. This, coupled with the subsequent decades of difficulties in gaining employment in a prejudiced society, has been a driving force in the level of community poverty we see today and the subsequent related problems that lack of wealth can lead to.

The lack of support was one thing; however, there was also a more sinister side of active prohibition that was also seen in many places in the Americas and beyond. For example, look at the sanctions, tariffs and punishments placed on Haiti for its achievement in becoming the first country to successfully expel slavery through rebellion.[15] The French, who controlled the Caribbean Island at the time were unsurprisingly angry with losing control of such a lucrative asset and, I suspect, the perceived embarrassment at being defeated in a military campaign by mere slaves thought to be inferior to their Caucasian masters. Large financial sanctions were placed on Haiti for their impudence of gaining freedom.[16] Haiti remains a drastically underdeveloped country today, partly for this reason.

This story of punishment for freedom was also seen in the US. The freed enslaved people were charged to work the land as sharecroppers, having in many cases to pay off the debt of their freedom[17]—the reality being not so dissimilar to their prior status as enslaved people. Again, these financial anchors placed on a supposedly emancipated people and the continuation of this through the nineteenth and twentieth centuries are a key reason for the levels of poverty we see amongst the Diaspora today.

Talent: Playing Catch Up

Within all groups of people, you will typically see a varied pool of talent. If you take a class of 30 children, the likelihood is that there will be around 5 who are not so academically gifted, around 20 who are average, and another 5 who excel. In statistics, this is what would constitute a bell-shaped curve or normal distribution.

A factor that is all too often dismissed is the genetic engineering that took place during the hundreds of years of bondage. A Mendelian approach was taken to the breeding of chattel enslaved people. There were two key pillars to this process. The first was simple: attempt to breed the strongest enslaved people with other physically superior enslaved people to create uber-enslaved people capable of being even more productive in their respective fields. The second was a more sinister policy of stunting intellectual development.[18] This consisted of killing enslaved people that seemed to be too clever and preventing the wide distribution or promotion of reading. The most an average enslaved person would get, if they were lucky, was a look in the Bible, and in some cases, even that was restricted to a select few.

What is the impact of centuries of intellectual suppression? Well, it is hard to formally test, but aspects of intelligence as with other attributes have a genetic link, so at the very least, you could not expect newly freed enslaved people to master investment strategies or debate the works of Plato when many could not even read! At the very least, the centuries of this type of setback will take a while to rectify with all things being equal. When you add on the additional barriers that were in place, for example, lower quality segregated schools, you can imagine the impact it has on the people of today. There is also a very literal cultural legacy of this type of policy in the progress of people and the cultural impact that can be created. If I look at my background as a Jamaican and compare some of our cultural norms with those seen in a Nigerian household, I can see that the focus on education is less. I believe the roots of this loss of cultural ambition are linked back to slavery. Looking at the average level of financial literacy among people in the Diaspora today, a link can be made.

While many aspects of the legacy of slavery can be found today, from colourism within the community to persecution from outside of the community, perhaps the most important is the economic legacy—a legacy of poverty and lack of generational wealth for those in the Diaspora. Let's find out more about the economic side of things.

Making Things Better

It is impossible to go back in time and change history, but we can learn from past mistakes and try to correct them. As we have touched on, and will see moving forward, there are still many legacy issues impacting contemporary times that we need to solve. As we explore the present-day challenges, we will identify opportunities to overcome them.

The Interconnectedness of History

A key theme of this book is the interconnected nature of the different aspects of the world we live in: how it is important to not view respective individual challenges faced by the Diaspora in isolation as they are often strongly connected and influenced by other issues in society. Much like the economic foundation that we will go on to discuss, history is also a basis that shapes our present-day realities. There are many legacy issues based on racism, oppression, and White supremacy that still impact us today—from police brutality and mass incarceration, to disparities in healthcare and housing. In recent times, we have seen 'modern' Western political narratives attempt to clamour to bygone periods that were much more difficult for those in the Diaspora. After all, the past, present and, worryingly, future are one and the same if nothing changes.

Chapter 3: Economic Anchors

'Economics is everywhere, and understanding economics can help you make better decisions and lead a happier life.'[19]
– *Tyler Cowen*

'I had to make my own living and my own opportunity. But I made it! Don't sit down and wait for the opportunities to come. Get up and make them.'[20]
– *Madam C. J. Walker*

In this chapter:

Challenges/context

- An overview of the financial state of the DiasporaObstacles to generating wealth e.g. lack of ownership, homeownership and types of employment
- Barriers to building businesses

Making things better

- Increasing ownership and entrepreneurship

- Liberating capital
- Building business networks and driving mentorship
- Diversifying forms of employment and business
- Smarter use of resources and investment strategies

Money is the Root of All Evil

I personally believe there are more important things in life than money, but I can't deny that it is important to a degree. I don't believe money can buy happiness; however, it can bring a level of comfort. Moreover, a strong economic base can alleviate critical concerns and make life easier. Finances can provide access to better education, healthcare, and safer housing—all key aspects for survival and flourishing. In addition, more disposable income can enable you to enjoy the more materialistic parts of life that we tend to overemphasise in the modern world. As we have seen from the review of Diasporan history, there was limited opportunity for wealth to be created and passed on, and practically no chance to experience the securities that can come with wealth.

Building a House on Weak Foundations

As you probably know, the man who tried to build his house on sand didn't fare so well. Like building a house, a strong economic base is the foundation for the progress of any group of people in society and society as a whole. A strong economic foundation is the backbone of liberation and independence. It is the basis of self-reliance, influence and bargaining power. A strong financial platform facilitates a comfortable life, offering the means to provide for your family through well-paid employment. However, the economic foundation that people of the African Diaspora have based their journey of development on is a weak one. As mentioned, there was no opportunity for wealth creation during slavery, and minimal opportunity during the Reconstruction period and civil rights era. This continues through to the present-day reality where we see a lower wealth base for the African American community compared to other ethnic groups.

There are a few damning statistics that illustrate the economic health of the Diaspora. These are perhaps most stark when looking at the wealth disparity between African Americans and White Americans.

Poverty statistics:

- Black Americans are more than twice as likely to live in poverty as White Americans (19.5% vs. 8.2% in 2020).[21]
- Black children are three times as likely to live in poverty as White children (26.5% vs. 8.3%).[22]

When assessing broader wealth measures in regards to the accumulation of assets e.g. property, stocks and other assets of financial value also shows that African Americans are worse off than those from other races:

- The typical Black household earns a small fraction of a White household—just 61 cents for every dollar.[23]
- The median annual household income for Black households in 2018 was $41,692, more than $21,000 less than the average for all households and nearly

$29,000 less than White households, which had a median income of $70,642.
- In 2016, the median wealth of Black families ($17,000) was less than one-tenth that of White families ($171,000).[24]
- In the US, overall, 86% of all households in the top two quintiles of income (upper-middle incomes are over $55,331) were headed by someone identifying as White alone, while 7.21% were headed by someone who identified as Hispanic and 7.37% by someone who identified as African American or Black.[25]
- Households headed by Hispanics and African Americans were not only under-represented in the top two quintiles (fifths), but also overrepresented in the bottom two quintiles. Whites were relatively evenly distributed throughout the quintiles, only being under-represented in the lowest quintile and slightly overrepresented in the top quintile and the top 5%.[25]

Homeownership, another important indicator of wealth, is also lower in the African American community:

- Less than half (42%) of African American families own their homes compared to almost three-quarters (73%) of White families.[26]
- There is a significant decline from the peak African American homeownership rate of 49% in 2004.[27] The collapse of the housing market in 2008 hit African American homeowners particularly hard, with Black

households over 70% more likely to have faced foreclosure than non-Hispanic White households.[28]

Employment statistics are not much better:
- Over the past 50 years, the unemployment rate for Blacks has been consistently twice that of Whites. Former President Trump proudly announced that the Black unemployment rate had dropped to 6% in January 2020; however, it was still double the White unemployment rate of 3.1%.[29]
- Ironically, college-educated African Americans face a larger absolute income gap compared to White Americans, compared to the gap seen with both groups without a college education.[29] It would seem that the boost of a college education is not always an advantage. Those with less than a high school education earned around $3,500 less than their White counterparts whereas college graduates maintained a gap of $11,000.[29]
- Racial wealth disparities are larger for more highly educated African Americans and Whites than for those with less education. While the African American-White gap in wealth was $51,000 for those with less than a high school education in 2016, for those with a bachelor's degree or higher, the gap was over $300,000.[29] The median net worth of college-educated Black families was $68,200, while for White families it was $399,000.[29]

These statistics make for pretty clear reading. African Americans have lower income and less wealth than other ethnicities. This trend is also observed across the pond. The average household income in the top 25% of Black Brits (British) was less than half of that of Whites and almost 50% less than Asians.[30] In addition, the number of Black Brits in the lowest quartile of earners was almost a third higher than their White counterparts.[30] Black British people represented the smallest proportion of the richest Brits and the largest portion of the poorest Brits.[30] These numbers are a strong indication of the earning disparity in different ethnic groups. These are the facts, but it is important to get a better sense of what has contributed to this state of play.

Barriers to Generating Wealth

Banking and homeownership

Why is the Black community at the bottom of the respective economic league tables? In truth, it is a combination of systemic discrimination and the subsequent impact of these barriers. As we have seen through a historical lens, Black people were not able to accumulate wealth through the bondage of slavery. Then, during the Reconstruction period, the dominant industry was sharecropping, which in effect was de facto slavery, and so wealth generation was near impossible. The Jim Crow era of segregation, particularly in the early twentieth century, afforded a short period of economic prosperity, but even in those relatively fleeting moments of success, for example, with Tulsa and Black Wall Street, we saw that the creation of independent Black wealth was met with White domestic terrorism and destruction; an entire community razed to the ground at the hands of oppressive Whites.[31]

The traditional way to build wealth is through homeownership, building up equity through the appreciation of a home's valuation over time. Subsequently, larger, more expensive homes are bought over time and the equity of the assets is passed on to the next generation, giving them a significant 'leg-up' as they go about their own wealth-building journey. It is a common story in the West for parents to give their children deposits so they can buy their first home and get on the property ladder, immediately moving from lost income in rent to asset growth with a mortgage.

However, following the Great Depression, this journey was not so straightforward, even for White Americans. As part of Franklin Delano Roosevelt's New Deal, federal policies that enabled White Americans to purchase homes through government-backed loans were introduced; however, African Americans were excluded and prevented from participating in this pivotal wealth creation opportunity.[32]

The exclusion from federally backed mortgages was coupled with exclusion from the banking sector and access to loans, which led to the rise of Black-owned banks. On the surface, this level of financial autonomy should have been a great thing, despite its relatively small scale. At its peak in 1926, Black banking controlled about $13 million in assets, which was about 2% of all US banking assets at the time.[33] The rise of Black banks was sadly halted by the Great Depression, and subsequent ventures fell victim to negative financial cycles. Retail banks work under the premise of fractional reserve lending to create the magic multiplier effect. This means a portion of whatever funds deposited by customers are loaned out to other customers to make interest and profit for the bank. Ideally, banks will loan out large amounts from deposited funds to allow them to make greater profits. In theory, a bank has to have a certain amount of funds readily available or liquid to satisfy the needs of a customer at any given time—how would you feel if you put money in your card in the machine and could not access your hard-earned money?

African Americans being poorer customers and more likely to withdraw their funds, meant more money needed to be available at any given time. The need for higher liquidity meant that less money would be available to loan out or invest, making these Black-owned banks less profitable. Less profitable banks had fewer resources to potentially loan to customers who were largely looking for loans to buy homes and build wealth, and so the cycle continued…

An additional problem was with the type of loan that was being requested. By and large, the majority of loans were mortgages and not business loans. This was problematic because of the racially biased housing market. Segregation at the time was legal and ruthlessly enforced. African Americans attempting to buy homes that were not in the ghetto were held back by higher prices based on White sellers not wanting to sell to Black buyers. If they could afford the premium prices, the assets usually lost value because neighbouring Whites would move away because of race-based discrimination and fear of depreciating assets—thus a self-fulfilling prophecy was driven by those who left, creating less *desirable* neighbourhoods because there were fewer White residents. As more African Americans moved into an area, more White people left ('White flight'), subsequently driving down the value of the homes in the area. So, Black banks had assets that were depreciating in value over time and Black homeowners were losing equity on homes they overpaid for in the first place!

In truth, the Black banks were fighting a losing battle in a segregated world. As Whites owned all the property, money was consistently leaving the Black community and not being recirculated. Black buyers paying White sellers facilitated the flow of money into the White banking system, a flow of money that would never come back to the Black community in any meaningful sense. White buyers would never buy from Black owners, and if the owner and seller were Black, at some point in the chain, the financial resource would leave the Black community.

Housing following segregation

Fifty years after the passing of the Fair Housing Act that prohibited discrimination in housing sales, rentals, or financing based on religion, race or national origin, residential segregation is still widespread in the US. Throughout the 51 metropolitan areas in the US with at least 1 million residents, the average segregation index was still nearly 60—where 0 represents full integration and 100 represents the complete separation of racial groups.[34] Homes in majority Black neighbourhoods are valued at $48,000 less on average than homes in neighbourhoods with few or no Black residents, even when controlling for home quality and neighbourhood amenities.[35]

During the housing boom of the early and mid-2000s, Black loan applicants living in majority Black neighbourhoods were more likely to receive high-risk and high-cost mortgage terms than those living in majority White neighbourhoods. Research shows that Black applicants of a similar age, employment history, and credit score, seeking to purchase a home in a similar metro area, were almost 78% more likely to have a high-cost mortgage than White applicants.[36]

The millennial Black-White homeownership gap substantially exceeds that of every previous generation of Americans since World War II. The African American homeownership rate is lower today than it was in the 1960s.[37] White homeownership has stayed close to 70% in the past 40 years, while fewer than half of African American families own homes.[38]

The take-home message is that the 99th percentile Black family is worth a mere $1,574,000 while the 99th percentile White family is worth over $12 million.[39] African Americans, while constituting just under 13% of the nation's population, collectively own less than 3% of the nation's total wealth.[40]

Entrepreneurship and business ownership

Another key way to generate wealth is through entrepreneurship and business ownership. This is ultimately at the heart of the capitalist society we live in. Also, being your own boss gives you autonomy and independence in your vocation, which is empowering and has the potential to yield the biggest financial rewards. If you look at the vast majority of millionaires and billionaires outside of exceptions like royalty, they are all business owners, whether it be Jeff Bezos, Elon Musk or Bill Gates. Business ownership can create the capital needed to expand and create business empires made up of multiple ventures. If we look at Mark Zuckerberg, for example, he acquired Instagram and WhatsApp, complementing his original business—Facebook.

Unfortunately, the Black community in America has struggled to make large inroads in the field of business ownership. Data from the US Small Business Administration indicates that, of the 17.7 million minority employer small businesses operating in 2017, Latin Americans come in at around 5.6% or 322,076 businesses, with African Americans owning around 2.2% or 124,004 businesses.[41] However, the sales and employment numbers show a more troubling image—the 19 million White-owned businesses account for 88% of all sales and control 86.5% of employment in the US, whereas Black businesses account for only 1.3% of sales and a paltry 1.7% of employment. Latin businesses sit at 4% of sales and 4.2% of employment.[42]

Businesses that have the largest economic footprint tend to be those that also have employees. Sales from businesses without employees are significantly lower: 67.3% of firms without employees had annual sales of less than $25,000.[43] Any profits these firms made—if they did make profits—would only be a fraction of the total sales. Conversely, a majority (57.9%) of businesses with paid employees had annual sales of more than $249,999.[44] It is more likely that these larger businesses with paid employees are earning significant profits for their owners.

In 2020 alone, 41% of Black-owned businesses have been forced to permanently close their doors, compared to less than 20% of White-owned businesses.[45] Black-owned businesses are more likely to be in the sectors of the economy hurt the most by global health crises, such as food, retail, or accommodation industries.[46]

Barriers to Black-owned business

Those Black businesses that do manage to make it off the ground face challenges. Some of the main hurdles in the way of the Black entrepreneur are capital, network, and access to expertise.

Capital

- Small and larger Black businesses report problems obtaining credit. This is despite applying for funding at a rate 10% higher than non-minority counterparts. Black businesses are 19% less likely to be approved for a loan.[47]
- Black entrepreneurs are three times as likely as White entrepreneurs to say that a lack of access to capital negatively affects their business's profitability.[46]
- Start-up capital is important in the long-term success of a business, but Black businesses are often starting with less: around $35,000 vs. $107,000.[46] This can often lead to higher levels of debt; around 30% of Black-owned businesses spent more than 50% of their revenues servicing their debt in 2019.[46]
- This lack of capital occurs even though the requirements for Black applicants are more stringent. In one study, 73% of Black loan applicants were asked to provide financial statements for their businesses, compared with 50% of White applicants

with comparable profiles.[46] In addition, 31% of Black applicants were asked to provide their personal W-2 forms (tax statements), while White applicants were not asked.[46]

Less access to networks

– Black businesses are often starting with smaller professional networks to help build their businesses. This lack of support from experts in supporting fields makes the chances of success significantly lower.

Types of Employment

Public sector employment

Another challenge in terms of wealth generation is the type of employment that people in the Diaspora normally have. African Americans and Black Brits are typically employed in sectors that are lower paid and much more often in public sector work, which is lower paid than the private sector. In the US, there is also an issue of geography; the majority of African American workers are in the South, which is not where the highest paying jobs are located.

African Americans are overrepresented in the lowest-paying jobs and under-represented in the highest-paying jobs.

In the private sector, Black workers are more often found in industries that pay the least, industries with a large frontline presence e.g. healthcare, retail and accommodation. These industries also have some of the highest shares of workers making less than $30,000.[48] In retail, 73% of Black workers fall into this category. In accommodations and food service, that share is 84%.[48] Conversely, Black workers are under-represented in industries such as information technology, professional services, and financial services—all sectors that typically have relatively higher wages and job growth.[48]

The picture in the UK is quite similar: Black workers had the highest percentage of any ethnic group working in public administration, education and health (43.6%).[49] When Black people do work in the private sector, they struggle to progress to managerial and senior managerial positions. Analysis shows that companies hire Black employees for frontline and entry-level roles, but there is a significant drop off at senior management levels, with only 4%–5% of Vice Presidents and Senior Vice Presidents being Black.[48]

Again, we see a similar picture in the UK where Black employees hold just 1.5% of top management roles in the UK private sector—a figure that has increased by just 0.1 percentage points since 2014.[50]

Making Things Better

Growing an economic base is fundamental to the progress of any group, particularly the African Diaspora who currently have the lowest financial resources. We need a stronger economic base so we can support more of our own industries and businesses and become less dependent on others. This is not only critical for making practical shifts e.g. more jobs, better access to healthcare, improved access to higher education and reduced crime, but also in terms of shifting political agendas and mounting more systemic change. If we look at the progress made by other minority groups, much of this it is optimised and leveraged by economic strength and influence. It is very easy to ignore a group with a small economic base or a group that does not know how to effectively leverage its base. They are inherently less threatening to the system and have a lower risk if they are not appeased. So, how do we go about building this base?

Increase Ownership and Entrepreneurship

The first key area of expanding our economic base in the community is to increase levels of business ownership. There is a relatively straightforward logic that suggests if a group of people are heavily responsible for a product, they should have at least proportional representation at the level of ownership. Instead, you have a rather contrived farm-like mentality of cows making the milk and farmers making the profit, or more accurately, a slave- and master-style relationship of enslaved people picking the cotton and the farmers benefiting from the proceeds – albeit well-paid enslaved people. A prime example of areas of ownership we need to improve is industries in which we dominate, particularly certain sports.

If we look at the major sports in the US that are predominantly made up of African American players, e.g. the NFL and the NBA, and compare that to the number of owners (and also managers/coaches), we see a significant and problematic disparity. The NBA in 2020 was composed of 74.2% Black players and 16.9% White players.[51] Robert Johnson of the Charlotte Hornets was the first Black-majority team owner in the NBA in 2002.[52] He was technically succeeded in 2010–11 by Michael Jordan. In 2013–14, Jordan and Sacramento Kings' owner Vivek Ranadivé, who is of Indian heritage, marked the first time in the history of major pro sports leagues in the US that there were two non-White majority owners in a league. At the start of the 2014 season, NFL surveys revealed that the league was approximately 66.9% African American or mixed race and about 24.9% White.[53] There are no African American owners of any NFL team.

The music industry is slightly better but still needs much more improvement. How many African American owners of major hip-hop labels are there? A handful at most. We have the standout examples of Jay-Z and P Diddy, but in general, it is far too low.

Some artists are starting to become more business savvy, not being sucked into exploitative 360-degree deals that enable labels to profit from all proceeds generated by an artist, even if they are not music related. New artists now understand the importance of owning their masters. They are becoming more circumspect about the types of deals they sign, if any at all. This comes with the growing understanding that in the modern era, much of the work previously attributed to a label can be done independently; for example, promotion can be generated on social media platforms. This type of approach is resulting in an increased number of artists signing distribution-only deals or deals based on touring only.

One of the most obvious opportunities for economic growth and ownership is the hair industry, particularly products that are heavily consumed by people of African descent. I'm talking about everything from wigs to weaves, hair grease to hair wax, and everything in between. These are products where we are far and away the main consumer, yet our level of ownership is remarkably low. Mintel values the Black haircare industry at more than $2.5 billion,[54] and that statistic doesn't include products such as hair accessories, wigs, or electric styling products. Black consumers aren't just spending on products created specifically to appeal to them; in fact, in dollar terms, African Americans also spent considerably more money in the general beauty marketplace. Black shoppers spent $473 million on haircare (a $4.2 billion industry) and made other significant investments in personal appearance products such as grooming aids ($127 million out of $889 million) and skin care preparations ($465 million out of $3 billion).[55] African Americans make up around 13% of the US population but have outsized influence over spending on essential items such as personal soap and bath needs ($573 million), feminine hygiene products ($54 million), and men's toiletries ($61 million).[55] There are clear opportunities being missed here. No other ethnic group has such consumer dominance in a particular market with such a low level of ownership or return. This is even more striking when considering that the African Diaspora is often one of if not the poorest demographics in a given Western country. Currently, a dollar circulates in Asian communities for a month, and White communities 17 days.[56] How long does a dollar circulate in the Black community? Just 6 hours!!![56] African American buying power is at 1.1 trillion, and yet only 2 cents of every dollar an African American spends in this country goes to Black-owned businesses.[57]

The importance of ownership and resourcing is also associated with the power to improve social issues. Look at the story of Colin Kaepernick, the NFL player who was 'Blackballed' or ostracised for his peaceful protests against police brutality towards African Americans. Kaepernick chose to kneel during the US national anthem at the start of each game. Unsurprisingly, people who were against his protest tried to misdirect the basis of the peaceful protest, accusing him of being unpatriotic and disrespecting soldiers who fight and fought for American freedom. This is despite the fact many veterans and active service men and women support his peaceful protest, understanding the true meaning of his peaceful protest. As a side note, there is an interesting discussion to be had about 'what is the appropriate way to protest?' Those who are against civil protests are seemingly against everything from rioting, activism, and celebrity endorsements to peaceful kneeling during the national anthem. If it's any consolation to Kaepernick, many who sacrificed themselves to help others from Martin Luther King to Muhammed Ali; the 1968 Olympic protestors were viewed with derision/contempt at the time and even assassinated, only to be venerated by the world years later, securing a legacy on the right side of history. Picking back up on the Kaepernick story, this is a great example of a lack of power due to a lack of ownership. Despite the NFL being 70% African American, there are no African American owners—nobody to support this worthy cause—no new team for Kaepernick to move to when the San Francisco 49ers chose to drop him. Moreover, fellow players were threatened with punishment if they chose to support Kaepernick in his peaceful protest, the threat not only from league owners but also from the former Commander-in-Chief himself, President Trump. The analogy of highly paid athletes being no more than pampered enslaved people is somewhat apt.

Lastly, we need to diversify our influence and expertise outside of these mainstay realms of sports and entertainment. Expansion into other industries is key to growth. We need to have more of a footprint in technology, energy, finance, and production industries, to name just a few.

Home Ownership

Increasing access to homeownership through schemes to help finance deposits is key to wealth-building. Homeownership and rising equity are fundamental ways families generate wealth and inter-generational wealth. This is not only one of the most common methods of wealth generation, it is one of the most efficient as it is an asset that can increase in value while you invest but also can double as a place of residence. Considering we all need somewhere to live, the likelihood is if you do not own, you will be spending on rent which is usually the biggest individual expense a person will have. This is a pretty obvious solution that most people would strive towards. It is important to acknowledge that getting on the property ladder is not an easy thing to do, particularly if you are not coming from a place of generational wealth, as is the case for most Black people. It can be hard enough to make ends meet and pay for bills, let alone save money for a deposit. As such, it is important that there is some form of government assistance to help bridge the gap for lower-income families who could be struggling to save enough money. We have seen some positive things in the UK, for example, the 5% deposit scheme.[58] In addition, it would be great if the banking sector would also consider more flexible lending arrangements for those with lower incomes, but of course, that is a harder sell for private initiatives who are more focused on creating profit.

Capital

Increasing access to capital is a key strategy to aiding the growth of any business, and Black businesses and subsequent wealth generation are no different. Other communities have greater access to capital, making it easier for their enterprises to be launched and maintained. Small business loans, tax breaks and government initiatives are important ways to provide the financial support needed to help burgeoning Black businesses.[46]

Policy

Policy changes in the public and private sectors that facilitate engagement and business growth from minority businesses, e.g. promoting supplier diversity, is another key strategy. Billions of pounds and dollars are issued in state contracts each year. Ensuring that a percentage of these is directed to minority businesses can help redress some of the imbalance. Likewise, this approach could be taken for private sector businesses.

Support from Within and Networks

With increased ownership, there needs to be more support from the community for these businesses, especially small businesses. This is essential to survival and growth. This is not to say that all money should be spent exclusively within the community—that is unreasonable, potentially divisive, and not viable—but a conscious mindset shift needs to occur that results in actively seeking out these businesses and proactively supporting them. All other communities, particularly minority communities, will actively support each other's businesses. How often do you hear a rapper refer to a lawyers or accountants from outside of the community, as if they are the only credible sources of that type of service? I have never heard a rapper refer to seeking out an African American, or Black, lawyer in a song. This self-limiting narrative has to change. Keeping the African American dollar in the African American community for longer and keeping the Black British pound in the community for longer is key to the growth of the demographic. Tools like the Black Young Professionals Network[59] and the Black Pages[60] make identifying businesses and services easier than ever; we have no excuse not to promote the support of the business within the community.

Creating Black business networks to help connect these businesses with expertise to help them thrive is also key. The Black Pound Day initiative in the UK is a good example of this. Swiss of So Solid Crew fame is the founder of Black Pound Day (BPD), an initiative aimed at helping to address some of this wealth inequity.[61] BPD is a monthly event dedicated to supporting Black Business, the mission aims to '…address the economic inequalities and imbalances affecting Black businesses and entrepreneurs in the UK and global diasporic communities.' On the BPD website and Instagram page, Black businesses are showcased in an attempt to help boost reach and drive customer engagement with a particular focus on the BPD of each respective month. In addition to championing Black businesses, BPD has gone into partnership with tech giant Google to help promote Black businesses online through three initiatives:

- Free listing on Google
- One-on-one mentoring with Google
- Live training with Google Digital Garage

Through the mentoring services, business owners can get support with online marketing strategy, social media campaigns and help setting up a YouTube channel, all invaluable online services. In addition to the Google partnership, BPD has also partnered up with Soho House for a year-long initiative that will enable free membership to Soho Works, as well as mentorship and support with social exposure.

Vocation

Redistribution of the workforce across more lucrative and varied areas, particularly in the private sector, will also help drive wealth generation. Of course, people should work where they feel most suited but being more mindful about where the greater financial opportunities lie is vital in the decision-making process. Interestingly, the concept of chasing after wealth is not new for the community when we think about the attraction to high-earning careers like footballer, actor, or musician, but these careers do not serve a large number of people. It's virtually one in a million to be truly financially successful in those careers. A more realistic approach is adopted by other communities that focus on less lucrative but more attainable careers like accountant, lawyer, and doctor.

In a world of growing technological disruption e.g. the growing use of Artificial Intelligence (AI), traditional trade roles e.g. plumbing will also increase in value. In a world that is evolving quickly, we are not limited to these more traditional roles—there are new opportunities being created every day—but we need to be more open (and better equipped) for these more attainable yet lucrative roles.

Afro Tech, New Technologies...The Age of Cryptocurrencies

We have discussed the importance of a more varied base of vocations that will enable larger growth of income and subsequently accumulation of wealth. An area of growing importance is the field of technology, not only because this area is and will continue to be high paying, but it is going to become ever more critical as the world becomes increasingly digital. Unfortunately, the tech industry, as with most others, suffers from drastic under-representation of Black people. This is clearly illustrated by the low level of representation in some of the world's largest tech companies, for example, Twitter reported only 6% of their staff were Black, while Facebook had 3.8%,[62] In the UK in 2019, Black people made up just 3% of the UK tech workforce—and less than 3% of UK technology company board members were from ethnic minority backgrounds.[63] Additionally, the rate of change in terms of increasing representation is very slow. A report looking at employee make-up between 2014 and 2018 of the biggest tech companies showed that Apple had failed to increase the number of Black employees, remaining at 6%, while Twitter, Google, and Facebook could only manage a

1% increase in that four-year time span, moving from 1% to 2% or 2% to 3% following their small improvements.[64]

While we need to increase diversity in the tech industry, we also need to maximise opportunities that are available within new forms of technology. Embracing and appropriately leveraging technology can be a great leveller. Tech is allowing us to tell our own stories through social media channels, providing new job opportunities and may even enable us to create independent currencies. As we move to a cashless society, the rise and importance of cryptocurrency will continue to grow. There are some great benefits of cryptocurrencies including greater security, faster transfer and decentralisation. There are also some potential benefits for people in the Diaspora, namely moving money away from FIAT countries and a traditional banking environment. The value of traditional paper currency is linked to a country's Gross Domestic Product (GDP) and inherently the strength of the country's economy, often weak in developing countries. This of course, means that most countries in Africa and the Caribbean are in a weaker position with low-value currencies. Increased use of decentralised cryptocurrencies that are not tied to any country may help to level the playing field.

(Genuine) Diversity Beyond Superficial Representation

Following the global shock that was triggered by the death of George Floyd, many businesses—large and small—decided to formally recognise the plight of racism and discrimination endured by Black people in the West. In the wake of the global protest movement that followed, many companies began to reflect on their position on race and discrimination, while also looking at the diversity in their own ranks, realising that the headcount was pretty monolithic. The call to action was broadly twofold: take a firm stance against racism and endeavour to increase the diversity of employees. This sounds great on the surface, but unfortunately, the commitment from some organisations to follow through properly was lacking and at worst, they were being opportunistic.

This lack of follow-through and opportunism is well-illustrated through more superficial forms of diversity adopted by many companies, that is to try to recruit more ethnically diverse employees at low levels of the organisation to appear multicultural, innovative, and forward-thinking while ensuring senior management and executive positions maintain the same un-diverse make-up of White, typically male faces as before. Many companies are following this model of portraying an external facade of genuine diversity e.g. ad campaigns filled with actors from minority backgrounds. There are particular industries, e.g. sports brands like Nike and Adidas (and others), that are profiting from Black culture; developing ad campaigns and products that leverage Urban music, and the culture in general, without giving back to the community who provide the inspiration.

It is worth noting that part of the problem is that the pipeline of diverse talent is pretty narrow because, prior to 2020, very few Western companies had any interest in developing it. So, the sudden decision to try to correct the problem quickly is not an easy fix when demand far outstrips supply.

I will go on to discuss the importance of representation in the world of media later, but it is important that representation and diversity not only exist but also that they are not kept to a superficial level—that does not benefit the community and instead is used exploitatively by companies and organisations for their own ends.

Better Use of Resources

When we have it, what are we doing with it? The common source of wealth in the African Diaspora is through high-earning sectors that are typically high profile and entertainment-based—careers in sports, music, or inadvertently linked to entertainment of some sort. These roles can generate large incomes but usually over a short period of time around 5 to 15 years. These jobs are great in terms of generating income, but all too often the resources are used poorly. How many stories have we seen of superstars losing all their money, from MC Hammer through to professional sports stars like football player Emmanuelle Eboué?

We see the wealth used to compensate for a former life of poverty spent on extravagant jewellery and fast cars, not regularly enough invested into assets that will mature like property or mutual funds. The psychological basis of this behaviour is interesting and deeply rooted in the history of struggle faced by many in the Diaspora—something that I will be discussing further later on.

It is not all doom and gloom. There are some great examples of wealthy members of the Diaspora using their wealth wisely, not only in terms of preservation and growth but also giving back to the community and helping others: celebrities from Killer Mike[65] with his Black banking initiative to Stormzy and his Oxbridge tuition fund;[66] 21 Savage with his financial literacy project;[67] and Nipsey Hussle had multiple community ventures, including attempting to tackle LA's gun violence, developing the community with new real estate and supporting Destination Crenshaw, a 1.3-mile open-air museum[68]. These are great examples of giving back, and there are many more. This needs to be continued, encouraged and expanded until it becomes second nature. The phrase 'We all we got' from the '90s' cult classic *New Jack City* is an important one. If we won't support ourselves, who will?

Group economics (people from the same community, sharing resources towards a collective goal) is not new; many communities practice this strategy. Italian, Asian, and other communities all use group economics. It is a form of self-preservation. Group economics was also used very successfully by the many thriving African American communities from the 1890s to 1920s (Tulsa, Oklahoma, Redwood, Florida and Wilmington, NC. were the three most popular; yet there were many others) in America. Collectively pooling resources to reinvest in the community is a necessity if poorer communities want to independently make larger investments in their neighbourhoods.

Increase Financial Literacy

One route to improve our use of resources is improving our financial literacy. On the whole, we in the African Diaspora need to collectively become more financially literate. I for one can attest to having a low level of financial literacy for most of my adult life: little understanding of interest rates, compound interest, assets vs. liabilities, bonds, or shares. I didn't know much about medium or long-term investment strategies or the concept of building an investment portfolio. Gaining a better understanding of how your money can work for you and creating streams of passive income is key knowledge for the middle classes and above. Save and invest, a sense of frugality and prudence with your hard-earned money, this is, of course, easier when you have a solid foundation to start with. Generational wealth has long been the springboard for many young people trying to make their way in the world, allowing families to support their children with the house deposit that enables them to get their first rung on the housing ladder or assist them with starting their first business. This is not the case for many people in the Diaspora, so it is on us to make that change and provide the next generation with that 'leg-up', which can be so important.

Our financial literacy now needs to increase to ensure that all the hard graft and financial creativity used to generate income is also used in growing it and protecting it. Part of this is taking the glamour away from frivolous spending. Let's create a culture where we see people sharing pictures on their Instagram of their property portfolio and not the new sports car that instantly depreciates/loses value after purchasing.

The Interconnectedness of Economics

Economics, income and wealth can determine many things from the quality of your healthcare, education and housing to your ability to distance yourself from oppressive forces. This is not surprising when we consider the broadly accepted idea that 'money makes the world go round', impacting almost all areas of life. The historically inherited and consistently perpetuated weak economic base of the Diaspora means we are at an even bigger disadvantage, having to play catch-up in a space we were fundamental in building for many Western nations. Our smaller economic base affects many social areas, making it more difficult to rejuvenate our neighbourhoods, harder to fund activities for our young people, and more difficult to improve the quality of education and healthcare. It means we have less capital to drive our own businesses and make investments to grow the wealth we have. It also means we do not own the industries we dominate, e.g. aspects of the music and sports industry, but instead report to others. This all makes it nearly impossible to shape our own narratives, another important connection. Ultimately, for those in the Diaspora, it also means we are valued less by residing governments—this is a key reason, along with weak geo-political influence, why other minority groups receive more favourable treatment. As stated previously, economics is so fundamental to most of our lives, there are very few areas that are not touched by it.

Now we need to take a look at the broader impact of this weaker economic position...

Chapter 4: The Impact of Economics – Socio-Economics

'The cost of liberty is less than the price of repression.'
– *W.E.B. Du Bois*

In this chapter:

Challenges

- The impact of low economic status on crime
- Socioeconomic impact on housing
- Socioeconomic impact on education
- Impact on health

Making things better

- Social benefits of improving income and economic standing

Economics and wealth are key factors in contributing to the progress of any group of people and society as a whole. As the theme of this book is the interconnected and interdependent nature of different sections of the world and facets of racism; economic factors are also heavily interconnected with practically every other area of life where we, the African Diaspora, face challenges. Underpinning this chapter is the intersection between race and class, with people in the Diaspora overrepresented in lower-income brackets translating to social issues. Economic constraints impact everything from housing to health, from education to opportunity. This impact is particularly pronounced in countries like the US where government (federal) support is limited. Private healthcare and private education are common backbones to longer, more successful lives globally. In comparison to countries like the UK with a stronger public sector, notably with the national healthcare system, the NHS, the disparities are less damning although still important.

Poverty and Crime

Lower income and subsequently lower disposable income will lead to pressures that can impact various parts of life, from the quality of education to health and to crime rates. If we look at the relationship between low-income levels and crime, we can see a clear connection—those with lower incomes tend to commit more crimes.[69]

A study by World Bank economists Pablo Fajnzylber, Daniel Lederman, and Norman Loayza found that crime rates and inequality are positively correlated within and between countries.[70] The correlation observed here is closer to causation—inequality leads to higher crime rates. This finding was supported by a study from the Mayor of London's office, which showed that three-quarters of the boroughs in

London with the highest levels of violent offences are also in the top 10 most deprived areas.[71] In addition, the same boroughs also have higher than average proportions of children living in poverty.[71] The logic to this is simple, if you have less of what you need to survive, turning to a life of crime to try and gain what you need can seem like an attractive or even necessary option. This is not to condone criminal behaviour but an objective assessment of human nature in difficult circumstances.

If you buttress this with the combination of a materialistic world where we are encouraged to venerate monetary value, with a system with fewer opportunities for those from poorer economic backgrounds, then the connection between poverty and crime becomes even stronger. Much of mainstream society is effectively saying that your intrinsic self-worth is linked to how much money you have; the more you have the more valuable and important you are, but there will also be a limited number of legal opportunities for you to obtain this significant level of wealth.

This finding is further supported by the theory on crime by economist Gary Becker, who also claims that an increase in income inequality has a robust effect on increasing crime rates.[72] Conversely, a country's economic growth (GDP rate) has a significant impact in decreasing the incidence of crimes, as a stronger economy typically has an ameliorating effect on poverty levels. The implication is that alleviating poverty has a crime-reducing effect.

The US, one of the most inequitable nations in terms of GDP per capita[73] and the worst in terms of income gap growth, also has the largest percentage of its population in prison compared to other industrialised democratic nations—

over 2 million people.[74] This is clear evidence of the connection between wealth disparity and crime.

As people from the Diaspora are often the majority of the poorest people in any given Western country, there is a higher likelihood of poverty-driven crime within this community. This dynamic is exacerbated by systems of mass incarceration and the prison-industrial complex, which we will discuss later.

Socio-Economics and Housing

Environmental products – homes and communities' environment

Our homes are said to be our castles and where our hearts are. They are usually where our loved ones reside, including our most personal spaces, bedrooms, and importantly usually contain all our belongings—suffice to say, homes are very important places. Socioeconomics also play an extremely important role in the houses in which we live and the subsequent communities we reside in. In short, your income will largely determine your housing options.

In the US, there are approximately 1.2 million households living in public housing units, and almost half (48%) of the people are Black.[75] In the US, the financial status of your housing or the community you live in can often have broader implications. For example, it may not only be that if you live in a poorer area that you are subjected to lower-quality housing; it may also impact the type of services and resources available to you in your community. In many parts of the US, funding of the public school system is directly tied to the tax base of the given area.[76] Therefore, if you are in a poorer area and, of course, inherently have a smaller tax base, you then subsequently have less funding for your public school system; therefore, your schools are likely to be of lower quality.

The majority of people from the African Diaspora live in social housing and are in the lower quartiles of income. As we have seen, there is a significant impact driven by the lack of wealth and lower income in key aspects of life, ranging from higher crime to poorer health. These pressures can also take a toll on communities and social structures.

A major challenge that faces many in poorer communities is the lack of community stability and increased crime, which are the by-products of poorer economic circumstances. This type of environment is the perfect breeding ground for gang culture and the street drug trade. It can be hard enough to achieve in life when facing the obstacles of poverty, but these challenges are exacerbated by the allure of a criminal life when other options seem limited.

Socio-Economic Status (SES) and Education

The connections between the economy and other factors in life continue with education. US research shows that children from lower-income households or poorer socioeconomic status (SES) develop academic skills slower than children from higher-income households.[77] For example, lower SES is related to poorer cognitive development, language, memory, and subsequently lower income and poorer health in adulthood.[78] This is likely to be caused by a combination of factors, with a clear one being that schools in poorer neighbourhoods tend to be of lower quality, under-resourced, and have poorer performance. As mentioned, this is particularly prevalent in the US where the local tax base often drives the funding for the local school system. Of course, we see similar dynamics in the UK despite schooling not being linked to tax funding—rather an inverse relationship can occur where better government schools drive up local house prices as parents vie for property in the catchment area. Lower academic achievement consequently can perpetuate the low SES status of a community with fewer graduates less likely to attain high-earning jobs or achieve a financial status that could be re-invested to uplift a community.

As further evidence for the connection between SES and achievement in education, we see in the UK that free school meals (an indicator of lower economic status) are correlated with lower attainment (5 A-C grades at GCSE) in core subjects including English and Maths.[79]

Educational resources

Another factor contributing to the impact of the economy on education is the potential lack of educational resources some lower-income families suffer from. A child's literacy can be linked to their home environment; if they are not exposed to adequate learning resources, this can limit their ability to develop.

Literacy gaps in children from different socioeconomic backgrounds can be detected before formal schooling begins. Children's initial reading competency is correlated with the home literacy environment, number of books owned, and parent's interest in reading.[80] Those from lower SES families are, on average, less likely to have experiences that encourage the development of fundamental reading skills, vocabulary, and oral language.[81] This is exacerbated as poorer families are less likely to have access to educational tools like computers, stimulating toys, or tutors to encourage literacy.[80]

Academic achievement and exclusion

Research consistently shows that lower SES is correlated with lower academic achievement and slower rates of academic progress as compared with higher SES communities. Children from poorer families begin high school with average literacy skills five years behind those of high-income students.[80] Children from poorer families also tend to perform worse in STEM (Science, Technology, Engineering and Maths) subjects. Furthermore, children from high SES backgrounds are eight times more likely to obtain a bachelor's degree by 24 compared to those from low SES backgrounds.[80]

In 2014, the US high school dropout rate among persons 16-24 years old was highest in low-income families (11.6%) compared to 2.8% in high-income families.[82] While in the UK, the Timpson review of exclusions in English schools shows that the permanent exclusion rates for Black Caribbean students, who are also regularly in lower-income groups, is three times that of their White peers.[83] However, in some parts of the country, the findings are dramatically worse, for example, in Cambridge the exclusion rate for Black Caribbean students is a massive six times greater than that of

White British students.[84] This stark disparity is also observed in multiple London boroughs with the exclusion rate in Brent being 5.9 times, Harrow 5.3 and Haringey 5.1 that of White students.[84] Importantly, the Timpson report states that 'low educational attainment and progress is closely associated with economic disadvantage and there is a disproportionate number of Black children living in poverty'.[83]

SES and Health

The consequences of high poverty rates are felt in different areas of life for those in the Diaspora, including health. Those in the bottom 40% of the income distribution are twice as likely to report poor health compared to those in the top 20%.[85] In the US where private healthcare is more common, almost twice as many African Americans do not have health insurance, 9.7% vs. 5.4% of White Americans.[86] The average American family spends around 11% of their annual income on health insurance, whereas African American families spend about 20%, a large financial burden, particularly when taking into account the known income disparities.[86] African Americans are over-represented as part of the population who receive US federal healthcare support, Medicaid.[87] This was expanded under Obama's Affordable Care Act to reach a greater number of people; however, this expansion was only voluntary in terms of state participation. The majority of states who chose not to participate were in the South where the majority of African Americans reside (58% as of 2017).[86] Appropriate coverage is important as it leads to better health outcomes such as earlier diagnosis and treatment. Despite the benefits provided by the expanded health coverage, there are still disparities.

These disparities that lead to lower quality and restricted access to care can contribute to poorer outcomes e.g. lower survival rates for conditions like diabetes, hypertension, Triple-Negative Breast Cancer (TNBC) and prostate cancer that disproportionately impact people in the Diaspora.[88,89,90,91]

COVID-19

Given the magnitude of the pandemic that engulfed the planet for two years, I would be remiss in not dedicating some time to how COVID-19 has impacted the Diaspora, particularly as the Diaspora was significantly impacted by the pandemic. Interestingly, despite COVID-19 being a virus and a clear health issue, the real problem seems more connected to the socioeconomic status of the Diaspora. Not too dissimilar to the idea of *Wall Street sneezing and Harlem catching a cold*, those of African descent often suffer not just because of racial factors but because of the socioeconomic factors tied to being in a lower-income stratum of society.

In the UK, Black African men died from COVID-19 at more than three times the rate of White counterparts of the same age,[92] Black Caribbean men at almost three times that of White men, with Black African women almost three times and Black Caribbean women at more than twice the rate of White women—significantly disproportionate figures again.[93] The reasons suggested for this stark disparity are around the jobs worked, that those in the Diaspora are more likely to work in 'dangerous' jobs, aka frontline care jobs such as nurses who would be directly exposed to patients on a regular basis. Another purported reason is connected to housing, with those from the Black community significantly more likely to live in multigenerational households including the elderly who are at greatest risk. If these vulnerable people do not have their own accommodation, then it is harder for them to be shielded from those who could have the virus. This, of course, is an issue of finances, with Black families more likely to have to share living space with older family members to save on resources. A further reason cited is those living in built-up areas are at greater risk, presumably due to population density in built-up areas. Again, this disproportionately impacts those from minority backgrounds.[93] Here we see the issue of substandard housing again intersecting with health, to increase risk.

Across the pond, the picture as ever is a similar one, with 179.8 out of every 100,000 African Americans suffering the largest mortality impact from COVID-19, 147.3 out of every 100,000 Latinos, 150.2 from every 100,000 White Americans, and 96 per 100,000 for Asian Americans.[94] Similar reasons are considered for this outcome as those seen in the UK: multigenerational households and living in built-up areas.

One of the key differences between the US and the UK is the health insurance situation. Of course, in the UK with our publicly funded National Health Service, there is a safety net for everyone. This, however, is not the case in the private US market, and with African Americans still representing the largest uninsured demographic at around 11%, they are at greater risk of not receiving the healthcare needed to keep them alive.[87]

It is worth noting that underlying health conditions like hypertension and diabetes that are higher in the Diaspora and can act as co-morbidities. These too can be traced back to poorer diet, stress, as well as other socioeconomic factors.

Making Things Better

As all of these problems are driven by income status and economic standing, improving and strengthening these will go a long way to ameliorating the challenges. We have previously discussed ways of increasing the economic base of the Diaspora e.g. increasing ownership, smarter use of resources, and more diversified employment sectors. In the next chapter, I will discuss in greater depth societal challenges not inherently tied to income levels.

The Interconnectedness of Socio-Economics

The socioeconomic challenges faced by the Diaspora are clearly inherently economic. However, beyond the economic, the impact of lower socioeconomic factors across various important areas of life like housing is connected to other issues e.g. homelessness, which significantly contributes to psychological and mental health strain. The connection between poverty and crime is a key driver for mass incarceration. Keeping the Diaspora in an economically weak position while limiting opportunities for progression and mobility primes young Black people for a life of crime. This is catalysed by overtly targeted policing that provides the perfect fuel for a destabilised and underdeveloped community. Socioeconomic status also impacts the quality of education and issues of exclusion that are also closely connected to the prison industrial complex and mass incarceration, which we will discuss in the next chapter. The challenges of the lower socioeconomic standing are then exploited through negative narratives perpetuated in mainstream media e.g. glamorising gang culture—again, different aspects that all connect.

Chapter 5: Society

'Not everything that is faced can be changed, but nothing can be changed until it is faced.'
– James Baldwin[95]

In this chapter:

Challenges

- Past and present health disparities and discrimination
- Educational issues including narrow curriculums
- Problems with housing, redlining and gentrification

Making things better

- Increasing access and representation in different forms of healthcare
- Creating updated and more globally holistic curriculums
- Building stronger curriculums

Society is an amorphous term; it covers everything from neighbourhoods to culture to ideologies and everything in between. Our society can determine what we eat, how we are taught, how we communicate, and how we have fun; it can effectively shape our lives. Here we will take a look at some of the social challenges that face the African Diaspora away from an economic context. Through a social lens, we will examine health, education, and housing in turn.

Health

The field of health is particularly close to my heart as I have worked in this area all of my professional life. It was a sector that appealed to me because it is all about helping people, something that is a core driver for me and, I think, the majority of those who choose to work in the space. Of all the different areas of life, dealing with health issues is the one where you would think everyone would be safe. The supposed primary objective of trying to make people better and the ethics that sit alongside lure most into a sense of security. After all, the profession of health is all about preserving life and fixing the problems that threaten our well-being—doctors take the Hippocratic oath, swearing to protect the patients they serve.However, we see that even the hallowed field of health is not immune from the disease of racism. This is perhaps not surprising when we recognise the interconnected nature of the world we live in. After all, doctors and nurses are people too. They have friends; they follow politics; they watch the news. They are not in a vacuum removed from society; they are also influenced by the conventions of the time; for example, past agreement that racial discrimination was okay. This is something we have seen clearly in years gone by, when perhaps you may expect to have seen it, but sadly, there are still examples of this discrimination in the world of medicine in more recent times and even still today.

A historic lens

Racial discrimination can be found in various aspects across the world of health and medicine. This pattern can be traced back to when enslaved people were used in medical experimentation, with little regard to suffering or the cost of life. James Douglas pioneered a new eye surgery; 4 out of 5 of his subjects were Black.[96] Enslaved people were preferentially used in genitourinary surgeries at the beginning of 1830; 30 out of 37 experimental Caesarean sections performed by Francois Marie Prevost were performed on Black people.[96] In the 1840s, James Marion Sims, often hailed as the 'father of gynaecology', tested his operating techniques on Black female enslaved people, often without the use of anaesthetic.[97] Among many now-famous innovations, Sims developed the vaginal speculum, a tool to help view the interior of the vagina more clearly.[97] In addition, he developed a technique to treat vesicovaginal fistula, which is a tear between the bladder and vagina caused by obstructed labour. Sims was also a 'slave doctor' and used many Black children in experiments for Tetany, a neurological disease characterised by convulsions and spasms, which were the result of significant deficiencies in calcium, magnesium, and vitamin D.[96]

The problems with race and healthcare are not limited to the antebellum period; we see its prevalence in the twentieth century and all the way to the present day. In 1932, the US Public Health Service initiated the Tuskegee Syphilis Study, a programme that promised free medical care to about 600 sharecroppers in Alabama.[98] It was claimed that the study was designed to investigate the progression of syphilis in Black men—a theory at the time suggested that the disease presented differently in Black people. On the surface, this may seem like a fair approach, testing a purported hypothesis; however, the deceit was evident; the study investigators claimed to be treating these subjects, when in fact there was no treatment at all. The subjects were lied to and their disease was allowed to progress under the false auspices of treatment. Confirming the true intent of the study investigators, O.C. Wenger, a senior Public Health Service officer in the programme is quoted as saying, 'We have no further interest in these patients until they die,' clearly not the declaration of somebody genuinely interested in healing.[99]

Eugenics and planned parenthood

Eugenics taken from the Greek word *eugenēs* or 'well-born' is the 'scientific' method from the early twentieth century that sought to genetically manipulate the human race so that more 'desirable' generations were born or not born. This was effectively translated into a race theory that aimed to remove less desirable races, i.e. those that were not White. Eugenics is often linked to Nazi Germany, and rightly so, many experiments were conducted in the pursuit of a purer superior Aryan race; however, what many people are not aware of is that the Germans were somewhat late to the eugenics party, basing much of their work on existing initiatives in the US.

Black women in the US are far more likely to have an abortion than any other ethnic group, accounting for about a third of women who undergo the procedure.[100] Planned Parenthood is one of the largest charities in the US and the largest provider of reproductive health services, including abortions for American women. The organisation was founded by Margaret Sanger, a eugenicist who aligned herself with White supremacist organisations such as the KKK.[101] Sanger is quoted as saying, '...the gradual suppression, elimination and eventual extinction of defective stocks—those human weeds which threaten the blooming of the finest flowers of American civilisation.'[102] In addition, while working on the 'Negro Project', a contraceptive initiative targeting the Black community, she has been quoted encouraging the use of trusted ministers to help influence the community, stating: 'We do not want word to get out that we want to exterminate the Negro population, and the minister is the man who can straighten out that idea if it ever occurs to any of their more rebellious members.'[103] Her story may be somewhat more complex as she was also connected to Martin Luther King and some civil rights movements, but the fact that she maintained views of eugenics in an era of prominent White supremacy, and also aligned herself with White supremacist organisations is damning enough.

Planned Parenthood, who supplies government-funded contraceptive pills, and other abortion clinics have operated heavily in African American communities for decades. This strong presence in Black communities is a significant contributing factor to abortion figures, with African American women making up 38% of all abortions in 2016 while making up only around 13% of the American female population.[100] Of course, it is imperative that women have choice and agency over their bodies should they fall pregnant; the issue at hand is the apparent focus of these initiatives in the Black community.

The Norplant contraceptive story from the early '90s is an example of clearly targeting Black women with a contraceptive implant. Thousands of young Black girls were part of roll-out for the implant, particularly those in Baltimore and New York. It was said that the high teenage pregnancy rate was the rationale, but these numbers varied nationwide and had been declining in the Black community. What is perhaps more shocking is that the implants could be given to teenage girls without consent from their parents, whereas children in the suburbs needed parental permission before receiving aspirin at school.[96]

Contemporary Medicine

As we look at the state of play in the modern era, we still see persistent issues of racial discrimination. A good example of this is the Human Genome Project. The Human Genome Project was the attempt to completely map the human genome, meaning that our genetic makeup could be decoded, effectively understanding the building blocks of what makes us who we are. It is described as 'one of the great feats of exploration'. Truly a mammoth undertaking, starting on October 1, 1990, and completed in April 2003, we were able to see 'nature's blueprint for us as humans'.[104] This is a pretty amazing achievement, but there was one big problem. The 'human' element only consisted of certain parts of the human species, i.e. predominately those of European descent, so the

Human Genome Project should really have been called the European Genome project. People of African descent were completely excluded from the study, despite making up a significant proportion of the human race and being the oldest known humans. This type of exclusion is typical of the way people of colour are viewed by people in the West, less important, missable, removed from the norm of Whiteness... even in a project with as comprehensive a title as the 'Human' Genome Project. Perhaps we are not considered to be human.

Under-representation in Clinical Studies

Clinical studies are the investigation of therapeutic interventions, e.g. medical treatments for different diseases and conditions, everything from arthritis to tuberculosis. Unfortunately, racial disparities are observed in many clinical studies today. It is more common than not to find clinical studies without any participants from minority backgrounds, and at best, they will form a small proportion of the study population being investigated. This is even the case in diseases where ethnic minorities are known to have a higher prevalence e.g. prostate cancer or Triple-Negative Breast Cancer (TNBC). Black men are twice as likely to get prostate cancer, compared to White men; they are also more likely to get more aggressive forms of the disease, and more likely to die from it, but despite all of these facts, they on average only make up 6.7% of the patient population in prostate cancer clinical studies.[91,105] TNBC is an aggressive form of breast cancer, which African American women are 28% more likely to die from, compared to White women.[106] The picture is similar in the UK with 22% of Black women having TNBC compared to 15% of White women.[107] Despite the drastic impact of TNBC on Black women, they make up only 1%–3% of clinical trial participants in the space.[108]

It is common to see less than 3% of most clinical trials include any representation from minority backgrounds, particularly African American or Black ethnicities. It is important to note that I am not talking about a proportional amount e.g. 10%–13% in America; I mean any representation at all, not even 1% of the genetic data available to inform new treatments – over 90% is from European ancestry compared to 1% of African ancestry and 2% of African American ancestry.[109]

This is all taking place against a backdrop of a world with rapidly changing demographics, where non-White populations will continue to grow, e.g. in Africa and Asia. In addition, large Western cities like London will continue to become more diverse in their ethnic demographic make-up.[110] We are also seeing the epidemiology of disease change across the world. By 2030, infectious disease will not be the leading cause of mortality in Africa, with incidences of cancer rising on the continent.[111] New cancer cases are predicted to increase by more than 80% in lower-income countries i.e. those countries with highest populations of people of colour.[112] By 2050, a third of all new cancer cases will be in China.[113] These populations will need treatments that historically have not been developed with these ethnicities in mind.

Under-Investment

We also see that race-based exclusion can be identified when we look at diseases that do not receive heavy financial investment. The notion of the 90/10 healthcare research gap is thought to exist, which articulates the disparity in how research funding is allocated, less than 10% of research funding is spent on diseases that impact more than 90% of the world's population. Diseases like sickle cell disease that predominantly impact minorities often receive the least investment.[114] A National Institute Health (NIH) study of US government funding, looking at sickle cell disease compared to cystic fibrosis, another genetic condition, showed similar levels of funding despite sickle cell being more prevalent (1 in 365 Black births vs. 1 in 2500 White births). The NIH should allocate funding depending on the impact of disease on society, but here we see an example of disproportionately low funding for sickle cell disease, with the key difference here being the communities impacted most by each disease.[115]

Race-Based Myths and Norms

If a clear reminder was needed of the present-day racial challenges faced by those in the Diaspora, we need look no further than the 2021 NFL cognitive impairment fiasco concerning African American players.[116] These American football players faced discriminatory cognitive evaluations based on their race and were subsequently denied financial pay-outs that they were entitled to.

Taking a quick step back for those who are not so familiar with American football; it is a very aggressive and dangerous sport, where heavy guys run full speed at each other causing frequent collisions with similar impact levels to that of a car crash. The average American footballer is 6'2 and weighs 111 kg. Suffice it to say after a career of these collisions, often being hit very hard on the head year after year, there is a high chance of cognitive damage in retirement e.g. dementia or Parkinson's disease.

Players are allowed to claim financial support if they can prove the cognitive impairment was caused by injuries sustained during their football careers. What transpired was a racially biased assessment, presuming the African American players naturally started at a lower cognitive level than White players i.e. African Americans are naturally less intelligent than White people. This lower starting point meant that African Americans had to demonstrate a greater cognitive decline than their White peers in order to receive compensation. This sounds like something from early twentieth-century eugenics theory but, somewhat astoundingly, was actually being practised in the present day.

It's not just professional athletes at risk of racial bias and misdiagnoses, it's everyday Black people too. As is a theme of the Black experience, racism can be everywhere, any individual can fall victim to it, even those entrusted with keeping us healthy. A survey of first and second-year medical students in the US showed that 40% believed that Black people had thicker skin and less sensitive nerve endings.[117] This is particularly concerning when you consider how academically talented and supposedly intelligent you have to be to get into medical school in the first place; these are supposed to be the best and brightest.

Risks with Medical Devices

If facing the challenges of discrimination from the people and policies in the world of health was not enough, there are also problems with the medical devices beings used. In 2021, it came to light that pulse oximeters, devices used to measure how much oxygen is in the blood, were overestimating the amount of oxygen in the blood of minority patients. The error was caused because the devices only worked effectively with fairer skin tones, placing minorities at risk.[118] These devices were often used as part of monitoring those with COVID, which as we know disproportionately impacted Black people. These misfiring devices serve to compound the biases and misunderstanding of Black people by healthcare workers putting us in even more danger.

Disparities in Maternal Care

Kamala Harris made a swift start to life in office by accelerating policy changes that could improve the lives of African American women. Harris' Maternal Care Access Act looks to address the huge race-based disparities in maternal healthcare.

What are the racial disparities in maternal care?

- Data from the Centres for the US, Disease Control and Prevention (CDC) show that Black women are 3 to 4 times more likely to die from pregnancy-related causes than White women.[119]
- There are 42.8 deaths per 100,000 live births for Black women, compared to 13 deaths per 100,000 live births for White women.[120]
- Black women in the US suffer from life-threatening pregnancy complications twice as often as their White counterparts.[121]

- High rates of maternal mortality among Black women span income and education levels, as well as socioeconomic status; moreover, risk factors, such as a lack of access to prenatal care and physical health conditions, do not fully explain the racial disparity in maternal mortality.[122]
- In the UK, in 2022 a task force to 'level-up' maternity care and tackle disparities was set up, following the acknowledgement that Black women are 40% more likely to experience a miscarriage than White women.
- In addition, researchers at the University of Oxford found that between 2014 and 2016, the rate of maternal death in pregnancy was 8 in 100,000 White women, compared with 15 in 100,000 Asian women and 40 in 100,000 Black women.[123] Black women in the UK are four times more likely to die from maternal death than White women.[124]

Why is this happening?

Systemic challenges and issues of implicit bias are at the root of the problem with maternal care. At times, there is an assumption that because doctors and other healthcare personnel are responsible for our health – that they are somehow naturally benevolent beings who are above or beyond discrimination or racial bias but, of course, that is not necessarily the case.

- A growing body of evidence indicates that stress from racism and racial discrimination results in conditions—including hypertension and pre-

eclampsia (a pregnancy complication related to high blood pressure and organ failure)—that contribute to poor maternal health outcomes among Black women.
- Pervasive racial bias against Black women and unequal treatment of Black women exists in the healthcare system, often resulting in inadequate treatment for pain and dismissal of cultural norms with respect to health.[125] As touched upon, studies, including a 2016 study by the University of Virginia researchers, found that White medical students and residents often believed biological myths about racial differences in patients, including that Black patients have less sensitive nerve endings and thicker skin than their White counterparts.[126]

On a systemic level, we see research shows a number of factors, including poor access to pre- and postnatal care, chronic stress, the effects of racism and inadequate medical treatment in the years preceding childbirth are all likely to play a role in a Black woman's likelihood to suffer life-threatening complications in the months surrounding childbirth.[125]

Transcending racial discrimination through wealth

Some people believe that racial discrimination can be avoided if you make enough money. There are, of course, many aspects of discrimination that intersect with class, which can be improved by moving into a different tax bracket. However, there are many instances where we see that the size of your bank account doesn't mean you can escape discrimination.

Interestingly, in maternal healthcare, we see that socioeconomics does not play a significant role in discrimination. A clear example of this is seen in the poor treatment received by Serena Williams shortly after giving birth. Serena, one of the most famous and financially secure Black women in the world, could not escape discrimination during her maternal care. Following the birth of her child Olympia, Serena who suffers from blood clot problems felt short of breath. She demanded a CT scan knowing she was no longer on her anti-clotting medication because of her pregnancy. The nurse did not listen to her concerns, deciding instead that her pain medication was making her confused. Thankfully, Serena was confident enough and strong enough to force the issue, leading to a scan which revealed blood clots in her lungs. If it wasn't for her agency and determination, these clots would have been missed and could have put her life at risk.[127] Another shocking example can be seen with the gold medal winning 4x100 USA relay team from the 2016 Rio Olympics; three out of the four woman team experienced health issues while pregnant, with Tori Bowie tragically dying during child birth. Again, it's important to reiterate that these are wealthy, physically fit women, who in some cases have an above average understanding of human biology and their bodies—most people don't have that; you can imagine what an average woman might face.

Education, Education, Education

Knowledge is power, an old proverb, which I believe holds a lot of weight. You can't really do anything unless you know how to do it. Conversely, if you know how to do many things, you have many doors open to you. The main port of call of knowledge is through our education systems e.g. schools and universities. In Western countries, these institutions are hailed as extremely important. I was going through my key school years under Tony Blair's New Labour government of the '90s, where higher education was pushed as an essential path to social mobility and success in general. But is this important and a key part of society serving everyone equally?

What Are We Taught?

Whitewashed curriculums

An issue with the current education system is the content, particularly from a historical perspective. In the UK and the US, there is no emphasis on world history. The history taught is largely focused on the events of the native country and perhaps Europe. There is a logic to that in that it is the country of study, why would you learn about Papua New Guinea? However, what we lack is the completeness of the history of these countries, particularly the UK in relation to its empire and impact around the globe. The UK once had one of the largest empires in world history, from Asia to Australia to the Caribbean. Britannia's reign was when the UK was most dominant globally, yet very little is taught about that time period and the countries involved in the Empire. It is where the majority of the country's wealth and influence was generated. However, the history of the British Empire is brutal. It is one of oppression and bloodshed; it is not pretty or glamourous in detail and as such is often whitewashed or omitted from history curriculums. These significant omissions cause many problems, particularly around immigration, where nationalists fail to understand the historical ties to many immigrating populations.

Critical Race Theory

It is said that 'History is written by the victors'. A mantra that some White Americans are looking to implement in full effect when it comes to the notion of 'critical race theory'. If a narrow and biased curriculum wasn't enough of a challenge, in the US, we currently see the concept of 'critical race theory' being questioned. Critical race theory (CRT) is the term used to describe any teaching that covers historical racism and discrimination perpetrated by White Americans, i.e. most of American history if you consider colonising the country from Indigenous Americans, slavery, segregation and the civil rights movement. This is particularly interesting considering many White people have pled ignorance about the challenges faced by Black people in the West. This ignorance is sought to be exacerbated by a group of White people actively saying, 'We don't want our kids to be taught about it'. Since January 2021, 37 states have been considering passing laws or have created initiatives to prevent this critical part of American history from being taught, with Tennessee, Florida, Ohio, and four others already passing the law. This number is likely to increase.[128,129] The suggestion that White Americans should not be taught about parts of history that make them look bad may be the epitome of privilege. Not only is it the fair and objective thing to cover American history as it happened, but it is also the right thing to do in terms of trying to build a better future. How can we learn from the mistakes of the past if we try to hide them?

A final consideration with the CRT narrative is its insidious use by certain groups as a means to reel back progressive education more broadly. The argument that the education system is leaning so far 'left' that the only way to balance it is by going extremely 'right' is a dangerous one. What many fair-minded people want is an accurate and fair reflection of history; to high-jack and position that goal as something that is extreme or unreasonable is misleading. As mentioned, to go a step further and suggest that the counter to an accurate portrayal of history is an inaccurate, white-washed version makes no sense at all.

Topics of interest

This is problematic because it means the focus of the historical study is around areas that may not be of interest to those from minority backgrounds. I would have been much more motivated to learn about Marcus Garvey than I was about Henry VII. However, everyone is obligated to learn about topics of Western interest or White interest. You could argue that in countries that are heavily dominated by people of that background, it makes sense, but it doesn't detract from the reality that the content is likely to be less compelling to those who do not identify with those figures.

A focus on negative narratives

What is taught is not only limited in scope but also negative in tone. When I was in secondary school, the only Black history I received was two weeks on transatlantic slavery. If I didn't choose to go on to study A-Level History, I would have been limited to the slave trade—that is the summation of the history of Black people. At A-Level, I was fortunate enough to have a module on American civil rights, but again it was limited in scope. This is problematic as it dramatically narrows the perception of the value contributed by people of colour throughout history, restricted to struggle and servitude. This is a serious issue for children of colour as it sets subconscious limits on what they can achieve and also for others in society who believe that Black people have not contributed to the world, which is patently untrue. It is tragic that despite all the challenges faced by people of colour in the Diaspora, there were still many significant historical contributions in all fields, from technology to sports to politics and beyond. To name but a few: Garrett Morgan who invented the tri-colour traffic light and the gas mask, James E. West who co-invented the electric microphone, Mark Dean who co-invented the colour PC monitor and the gigahertz chip, and Alfred L. Cralle who designed and made the first golf tees.[130,131,132,133]

Who Are We Taught By?

All members of society are subject to conscious and subconscious bias; we touched on this with regards to healthcare. Education and educators are no different; teachers read newspapers, watch television, converse with friends and family, and are subject to influence and prejudice. This is particularly important when we see the low numbers of Black teachers in the education system. As of February 2021, Black teachers make up fewer than 5% of UK teachers;[134] a massive 68,000 more Black and minority teachers would need to be recruited to reflect England's school student population.[135] The issue of under-representation among educators is reflected in the US with Black teachers making up around 8% compared to around 14% of Black students.[136]

Racist or biased teachers can seriously impact on how Black children are taught and how they are treated in schools. I remember negative experiences with some teachers in primary and secondary school. In primary school, I had two teachers who stood out as having an issue with me for no reason, presumably other than race. I was not a naughty student; I definitely fell into the category of children who favoured positive reinforcement. I always wanted to do well on my weekly spelling tests and was always profoundly disappointed when I didn't score full marks.

This context is important when I think about one of the few times I did get in trouble as a kid; and let's be fair, the majority of children will get in trouble now and again, but when I did, I was treated relatively severely. It was almost as if I had a marker against me: 'potential threat, this kid could be a problem, be careful'. This, of course, was not based on how I was as a student or my behaviour record. I performed well and didn't get in trouble often; it was something I can only ascribe to my race. By default, being Black came with a warning of trouble; I was immediately a heightened risk. It is this type of unfair conscious and subconscious bias that feeds into the harsh treatment of young Black boys and girls and the high exclusion rates—it is as if everyone else has three strikes and we only have one strike. In parts of the UK, exclusion rates are six times higher for Black Caribbean boys compared to their White counterparts. Across all demographics, Black and mixed-race boys have the highest rates of temporary and permanent exclusion.

The other aspect that stands out to me is perceived expectations—that is to say, low expectations. I personally experienced being tarnished with the lower expectation brush on two distinct occasions during my school days. The first occasion was at the end of primary school. At the end of primary school, you sit an exam. This exam is somewhat important because it determines if you can attend certain secondary schools. In this national exam covering the core subjects of Maths, English and Science, I scored average marks. As mentioned, because I was a child who sought positive reinforcement and affirmations, these average marks were not what I was hoping for; I was disappointed. In expressing my disappointment to my mum, she contacted my teacher to discuss the outcome. She was flatly told that I should be happy with these average marks. Now, this may seem slightly trivial because the average is where most people are, but it was more around the tone and messaging. It wasn't so much 'your child is of average intelligence so he should be happy', it was more 'average is a good place to be for a child like yours, a Black child'. Reflecting on this, I'm convinced that this is largely subconscious bias in action, the innate acceptance that average is good for a Black child—why would you want more?

The second time I experienced this attitude was in secondary school following my GCSEs and about to start my

A-Levels. At the time, the traditional science subjects, Chemistry, Physics and Biology were combined into two blocks called 'double science'. I ended up with a B as my grade for double science and wanted to take Biology as an A-Level option. Technically, you only needed a C grade to take a subject on at A-Level, but ideally, you would have a B or A grade. One of my teachers, who would then go on to be my biology teacher, greatly discouraged me from taking Biology at A-level, despite it being my strongest and preferred science subject. This conversation was a clear example for me of bias; despite my performance and grade, she did not see me as a science student. While other kids were being encouraged to take subjects or at worst receiving a neutral reaction and not a negative one, I had barriers put up against me in my pursuit of education. I would go on to get a degree and master's degree in Neuroscience from two of the best universities in the country, achievements I could have missed out on if I had listened to her discouragement.

Limited expectations and barriers to ascendency may seem like relatively small or ephemeral topics, intangible or inconsequential mindsets, but they have very real implications and impacts on our lives. As described through my own personal experiences, low expectations and not judging them on the objective merit they demonstrate creates barriers to progression. If your implicit or explicit bias cannot see a person of colour as CEO or leader, then it is going to be significantly harder for that person to achieve that. These unfair judgements still exist today in a world where one of the most inspirational world leaders of all time, President Obama, is a man of colour.

Exclusion Rates

Earlier, we looked at the disparity in exclusion rates between those in the Diaspora and other groups in relation to lower-income status. However, the stark disparity—up to six times higher exclusion rates in some parts of the country—is going to be driven by more than finances alone; after all, there are poor White students too[84]. The likelihood is, as in other areas of society, racial discrimination is driving harsher treatment for Black students—effective criminalisation by the schooling system. This is something that is closely tied to broader negative narratives and stereotypes that we will discuss in greater depth later. The longer-term impact on the life trajectory of those excluded has been shown to be huge, with exclusion not only seriously impacting academic performance, but even more concerning, it has been shown to be a path to crime and imprisonment i.e. the school exclusion to prison pipeline—which illustrates the key milestones many Black students follow.

The school-to-prison pipeline: sent out of class—detention—isolation—temporary exclusion—permanent exclusion—Pupil Referral Unit (PRU)—young offender institution—prison—re-offending.[137] This is a very effective slippery slope that is hard to get off once you've been labelled and entered the system. As we know, for many the labelling starts from day one. Students who are permanently excluded attend a PRU; this is a difficult environment that consists of only students that have behavioural challenges. Suffice to say it is difficult to be productive and get on the right track in that environment. The pipeline takes 85% of those in PRUs to young offenders' institutions (youth prisons); from there, there is a 70% re-offence rate, likely landing in adult prison.[138]

Environmental Products – Homes and Community Environment

We discussed some of the socioeconomic challenges related to housing and communities whereby poorer communities may be placed at a greater disadvantage through lacking other services because of residing in a poorer area e.g. schools with lower funding. You are probably familiar with images from 'the ghetto'; dilapidated buildings, drugs, gangs, violence, addicts, poverty and, usually, a majority of Black people. I remember a discussion with an ex-girlfriend's sister about the correlation between the Black community, violence, and poverty. She was under the impression that all Black people lived in poor areas because this was somehow objectively natural. Presumably, because she thought Black people were either, by default, too stupid to get good jobs to facilitate moves to better areas and/or inherently criminal, so destined to form gangs—or some other negative race-based notion that meant that substandard living was the only expected outcome; we deserved it.

On closer inspection, we see that the 'ghettoisation' of a people, in fact, practically any group of people who find themselves in that situation is usually because of outside forces dictating the outcome. Following the migration of millions of African Americans from slavery in the South in search of work in the North, we see that the discriminatory policy of 'Redlining' played a key role in creating these horrible living environments.

Before we get into the details of Redlining, we need to be mindful of the social climate at the time: the Jim Crow and segregationist mindset in America following slavery. White

Americans did not want to mix with African Americans and many of the key legislative steps of the civil rights movement in the '60s aimed to address these racist segregationist policies.

Redlining is a practice where certain communities are isolated or ring-fenced by a 'red line', effectively segregating that area and subsequently denying it from receiving important services, leading to the degradation and devaluation of the area. This practice was conducted in predominantly African American communities, meaning these residents would be denied bank loans and mortgages.

We still see examples of de facto redlining today. An article in the *Chicago Tribune* notes that African Americans and Latinos continue to be routinely denied conventional mortgage loans at rates far higher than their White counterparts.[139] It is reported that modern-day redlining persisted in 61 metropolitan areas even when controlling for applicants' income, loan amount, and neighbourhood, according to millions of Home Mortgage Disclosure Act records analysed by Reveal from The Center for Investigative Reporting. The year-long analysis was based on 31 million records, including data from the Federal Reserve and Department of Justice, to identify lending disparities. The study found a worrying pattern of denials for people of colour across the country, including in major metropolitan areas such as Atlanta, Detroit, Philadelphia, St Louis, and San Antonio. Perhaps unsurprisingly, African Americans faced the most resistance in the South; namely, Alabama, North Carolina, and Florida. This makes the problem more pronounced because the highest population of African Americans are found in the South. African American applicants reported similar stories of battles with loan officers who seemed to be looking for a reason to say no.

Frustratingly, these stories happen often. In 2016, Black loan applicants were 1.8 times more likely to be denied a housing loan than their White counterparts in Detroit.[140] The average denial rate for Black applicants in the Detroit metro area was 22% in 2016, a figure that significantly outweighed the denial rates of other minority groups.[140] This also included decreased access to insurance and healthcare protection as well as lower investment in community buildings. All of these help feed a cycle of poverty with depreciating community value that African Americans cannot escape from. To make the situation worse, law enforcement could target excessive and unlawful policing tactics, like stop and search in areas that have high numbers of African Americans. I will discuss the issues of policing in the Black community in more detail later.

This form of modern-day segregation is exacerbated by 'White flight', where White people actively leave areas that became 'too' populated by African Americans. This creates desirable and non-desirable areas to live in and continues to subject African Americans to poorer conditions.

Out of Sight, Out of Mind

The problems with segregated communities are not limited to the quality of local amenities and resources, it is also about how you can then be easily isolated and targeted. We see this with the way policing focuses heavy-handed stop-and-search efforts in Black communities. Sadly, we also see it with the treatment of Black communities in times of emergency. Back in 2005, Hurricane Katrina devastated New

Orleans and other parts of the Gulf Coast killing more than 1,000 people. It is said to be the largest urban disaster in modern US history; more than 110,000 homes and over 20,000 businesses were lost.[141] Black people, as is often the case, ended up worst off from the natural disaster, with 66% of Black people stating that the government response would have been faster if they were White. Moreover, only 19% of Black people rated the government response as excellent, compared to 41% of White people.[142] The racial disparities didn't stop at the quality of the relief effort; it continued in the regeneration process. Large poor Black communities like Lower Ninth Ward have not been rebuilt, while affluent White areas like Lakeview received a full upgrade.[141] Prior to Katrina, New Orleans had a large quarter of thousands of housing units known as the 'Big Four'; these buildings escaped with minimal water damage, yet city officials choose to demolish them anyway.

A similar lack of care and general humanity was observed between 2014 and 2019 with the Flint, Michigan water crisis. The city of Flint had its water supply contaminated with lead following a financial decision to change its water supply from Detroit-treated water to the Flint River. An example of finances being put ahead of public health. Flint is a majority Black city, with African Americans making up 57% of the population and White people only 34%. Furthermore, Flint is a poor city with 40% of its residents below the poverty line. This demographic make-up was the catalyst for the slow and haphazard management of the crisis that lasted for four years. It is also an important example of the intersection between race and class, which follows a similar path for many Black people in the Diaspora who as we know are often in lower-income groups. Many residents fell ill through consumption of the contaminated water, including some contracting Legionnaires' disease. A 129-page government report highlighted that historical, systemic and structural racism were key factors at play during the crisis.[143]

In the UK, we saw also the issue of isolation, segregation and neglect crystallised with the tragic Grenfell Tower fire in 2019. This tower block in West London was home to a predominantly ethnic minority community and had been left to fall into a state of disrepute, despite being located in one the most affluent boroughs in one of the richest countries on the planet. Flammable cladding had been added to the building to make it look more attractive to the richer neighbours; this cladding was the main cause of the scale of the fire. A reported 72 people died in Grenfell, a gross example of how the lowest in society can be left behind.

State-Sponsored Crime

Gang-related activity has been a consistent challenge of deprived communities all over the world irrespective of race, with the underlying driving factors here being poverty and lack of opportunity. However, in some cases, there are deliberate external factors that help to perpetuate this culture, particularly in regard to drugs, which is often the main source of revenue for many gangs. There have been various allegations of the CIA and other federal departments being involved in perpetuating illegal activity in the Black community, perhaps none more so than the facilitation of drugs to the community. A series of articles written by Gary Webb from the San Jose Mercury News accused the CIA of supporting the flow of cocaine from Nicaragua to Black communities in Los Angeles via legendary drug dealers Ricky Ross and local gangs the Bloods and Crips.[144] This is in no way to exonerate the illegal activity of these gangs, but you are really up against it when your own government is being accused of facilitating the pipeline to your neighbourhood. This flow of cocaine between the '80s and '90s is said to have played a significant role in the crack cocaine epidemic of the time. While multiple investigations into these charges came up with no clear evidence, perhaps unsurprising given what would be at stake reputationally, a broader question has to be asked about how and why drugs and weapons seem to so easily permeate poorer communities and often Black communities.

The COINTELPRO initiatives created and executed by the FBI are another example of negative state intervention in the Black community.[145] Documents show that the COINTELPRO programme deliberately infiltrated and aimed to neutralise a variety of organisations, including the Black Panther Party, which was conducting positive activities in the community–from education programmes to food assistance.

Gentrification – Where Did All These Coffee Shops Come From?

In more recent times, we see an inverted version of these segregated racial policies with the growing rise in gentrification. The areas once considered too poor and too full of minorities for White people to reside in are being bought back en masse as the demand for housing in inner city areas grows. The process of gentrification brings with it a lot of local rejuvenation because, of course, a certain living standard needs to be met for affluent White people to reside in the area. We are all familiar with the tell-tale sign of numerous coffee shops popping up and organic food stores where there were none before. However, the rejuvenation does not come thanks to the benevolence of housing developers looking to build a more integrated society. Quite the contrary, the same issue of segregation persists...many White people do not want to share communities with poorer people of colour, just as they didn't in the past. So, through the increase of rents, people of colour are priced out of the areas they were once confined to. From Brixton to Brooklyn, the process of extracting people of colour from formerly undesirable neighbourhoods is in full effect.

Chicken Shops and a Healthy Diet

The underdevelopment of poorer, often Black neighbourhoods can be characterised by the types of food shops present, namely the number of fast-food shops. There is usually a lack of affordable healthy food shops in poorer neighbourhoods, which is exacerbated by a plethora of affordable unhealthy fast-food options. Interestingly, this is almost the antithesis of what you see following gentrification where there is typically an influx of more healthy food shops (e.g. Whole Foods or Planet Organic) brought into a neighbourhood, along with the new White residents. The dominance of fast food outlets and lack of healthy shops has been termed a 'food desert' by those outside of poor communities. This choice of language is important because 'desert' implies that the unbalanced mix of food options in poorer areas is naturally occurring instead of the manifestation of systemic racism that it actually is.[146] As we have seen with redlining, certain healthy food outlets deliberately avoid poorer areas.

The food desert phenomenon was something I noticed a while back after realising that in England the 'chicken shop' (fried chicken fast food outlet) flourished in poorer areas. If you walk around any of these neighbourhoods in London or bigger cities in the UK, you will find them everywhere. What is particularly concerning is the number of young people from these poor areas who eat this stuff on a regular basis. At the end of the school day, these shops are teeming with hungry adolescents eating unhealthy food. Fast food on an infrequent basis is fine; the issue is eating it too often. While it is hard to say exactly how calculated this dynamic is, what we do know is that these shops are not present in more affluent areas. Similar to the US where gun and liquor stores only seem to be in the hood…it would be naïve to think any of this is an accident or coincidence.

Making Things Better

Health

In the healthcare arena, there is a lot that can be done to correct the equity disparities that are currently present. I will touch on a few aspects:

More inclusive research

We could be more intentional in the design and conduct of our clinical studies. We could make deliberate attempts to ensure that we have a broad representation of people from different minority backgrounds within the studies. This can be achieved through guidelines or policies from industry regulators e.g. the Food and Drug Administration (FDA) or European Medicines Agency (EMA). In addition, study sponsors and manufacturers, e.g. the pharmaceutical companies themselves, can set their own standards and targets that will ensure more inclusive research practice is brought to life.

In a similar vein, the types of diseases that are investigated could be re-examined. Pharmaceutical companies and regulators could make a more conscious effort to investigate diseases that disproportionately affect people from minority backgrounds e.g. sickle cell disease. The African Genome Project is also an example of this.[147] As discussed, the initial 'Human Genome Project' focused solely on those with European Ancestry, missing out on large swathes of the human population. The African Genome Project will seek to address this by mapping the genome of people of African descent.

Addressing maternal healthcare disparities

Implicit bias training

- Healthcare providers who serve pregnant women, including doctors, nurses, and midwives.

- Academic institutions, including schools and training programs described in subsection.
- Community-based health workers, including perinatal health workers, doulas, and home visitors; and community-based organisations.

Grant programmes

A grant program for accredited schools of allopathic medicine, osteopathic medicine, nursing, other health professional training programs, and other entities for the purpose of supporting implicit bias training, with priority given to such training with respect to obstetrics and gynaecology. More police-level work is needed in the UK.

A more diverse workforce

In the healthcare industry, as with most industries, we see a stark under-representation of people from minority backgrounds in the workforce. In the past and some cases still present, this was driven by discriminatory hiring policies and small talent pools. A way to increase the talent pool size is to provide scholarships to people of colour who show an aptitude for science but do not have the financial means to pursue science subjects at university. Training personnel, particularly hiring managers on conscious and unconscious bias can help to mitigate some of the challenge of discriminatory hiring practices.

We also need to see diversity across different layers of the organisation, not just at the individual contributor level. When the executive suite and senior management roles consist of the same demographics they always have, with only a peppering of diversity at the lowest level, no meaningful change has been made at all.

Education

A broader more inclusive curriculum

A key challenge is the myopic and whitewashed version of historic events taught in schools. This could be addressed with a revised curriculum that covers more world history but also provides a more transparent account of the exploits of the empire of Britain and other colonial rulers. This could also be extended to capture some of the tragedies of the twentieth century like the Tulsa riot of 1921 where 18,000 homes were burned, 304 homes were looted, and mostly Black people were killed and many more injured. The damage totalled between $2-3 million, a significant amount at the time. These more honest accounts of our history will help people better understand many of the causes of present-day challenges. The legal barriers being introduced in some American states to challenge critical race theory are a direct affront to creating a broader, more transparent curriculum. The Black Curriculum initiative is a great example of an independent education initiative that aims to provide a more comprehensive and transparent account of Black history to schools and anyone who is interested. Founded by Lavinya Stennett in 2019, the organisation has gone from strength to strength and has been recognised by several mainstream media outlets like the BBC, *The Guardian,* and CNN.[148]

Increasing knowledge of self

Another important avenue is increasing knowledge of self. Learning your history is key to combatting the negative stereotypes and narratives that are so widely perpetuated. As humans, we naturally imitate and adjust to our surroundings; it's key to our learning process, socialising and showing empathy. If all we see is negativity and know no different, our aspirations will remain low—it's hard to do better if you don't know better.

Knowing that you can be more than a gang member, because so many of those before you have managed to do so, is helpful motivation when trying to escape the trappings of a negative environment. A great example of this is the Pan-African Saturday schools that have been running in the UK for years. These schools focus on an Afro-centric curriculum, for example, the National Association of Black Supplementary Schools (NABSS), which is dedicated to highlighting, promoting, and supporting supplementary education to help *Afrikan* Heritage children and their families to get the best support for their educational and cultural needs, or the African Community School. This provides a great supplementary education to that received in the national curriculum, focusing on topics that would not usually get much attention but are key to developing self-esteem, promoting a positive mindset, and combatting negative stereotypes.

Transcending the trappings of a difficult social environment is not easy. This is made even more difficult when systemic barriers are in place, slowing your progression.

Housing and Community Policy

Anti-racist legislation

Legislation that combats clear discriminatory policies and practices like redlining is important. The Housing Act of 1968 and Equalities Act of 1964 are examples of how legal framework can be employed to protect people against these racist practices.[149,150] However, they need to be executed, as we have seen from the examples of modern-day redlining and the issues Black people have with mortgage denial—laws are often not enough. I think lenders should be regularly audited and have to justify any disparities in lending. Likewise, city and state government officials need to work harder to create more equal and less segregated neighbourhoods.

Building stronger communities

'The system'—the series of hurdles and traps that are in place for people of the working classes in the Diaspora—can be hard to transcend or circumnavigate. Being born into difficult economic conditions, with limited opportunities, poorer education due to underfunded schools, and growing up in neighbourhoods with higher crime rates clearly isn't the start that most people would want in life. With all that said, we still need to find a way to overcome these challenges.

I believe a mindset shift to an increased sense of community would go a long way to improving the situation. We could look at some of the positive work delivered by the Black Panthers in the US in the 1960s and 1970s; for example, the free food programme to ensure kids were not going to school on an empty stomach and providing protection for the community against an abusive police force.

This is not an easy fix. It will take the responsibility, time, energy and resources of people in the community to improve things. In Atlanta, we see a great example of this with the 'Buy Back the Block' Initiative spearheaded by rapper TI and Killer Mike, among other investors.[151] This enterprise is focused on buying African American neighbourhoods in Atlanta and redeveloping them for the community. This is a great way to give back, effectively gentrifying without the removal of the current tenants.

A strong sense of positive community is also important to help those who are lacking support. In 2019, African Americans accounted for up to 28% of single-parent households, disproportionately over-represented, while White households were underrepresented at 42%.[152] A similar pattern of over-representation can be observed with single-parent Black British families being around 24% compared to only 10% for White British families.[153] The old saying goes 'it takes a village' to raise a child; there is a lot of truth to that. Even if you are fortunate enough to come from a stable family, you can benefit from the wisdom and support of others. Of course, if you do not have a strong support system at home, you are in even greater need of an external support network. One of the biggest attractions to gang culture is the sense of being part of a family, having people that will support and protect you.

Mentoring

Being a mentor is a great way of providing support to people who need it and helping to build a stronger community. This can be as simple as an hour a week, taking the time to check in on a person, provide a sounding board, and offer some guidance. I have given up some of my free time to mentor those from more disadvantaged backgrounds. Helping teenagers to grow and develop, providing guidance and exposure to different options and potential career paths at an early age can be a huge boost for developing minds.

The Interconnectedness of Society

The problem of being underserved across different spheres of the societal realm, whether it's health, education, or housing, all have historical roots in the more flagrant discriminatory practices of the past, creating present-day permutations of those problems. We see the historical legacy of White supremacy in many of the social challenges that face the Diaspora today, from the world history that is being whitewashed in front of our very eyes with the banning of critical race theory to historical issues of redlining to reverse redlining and gentrification. We see the connection between Black people finding it difficult to access mortgages to the problems of lower-income status, and challenges generating wealth. The challenges of race-based norms and stigmas, driving an inferior perception of Black people as we see with the cognitive assessment of NFL players or the belief that Black people have thicker skin and less sensitive nerves are connected to the under-representation and lack of diversity in different industries. Black people are pigeonholed into certain roles based on unhelpful stereotypes. How can you have people of colour in leadership roles if there is also a belief that Black people are inherently less intelligent? The view of being 'less than' is also intertwined with the dehumanisation of Black people that regularly occurs. The dehumanised view that enabled the travesty of the Tuskegee Syphilis Study is the same dehumanised view that enables police offers to murder unarmed Black people.

As summarised above, there are clear connections between the social, socioeconomic and economic. Furthermore, it is clear that negative biases and under-representation of the Diaspora in most walks of life also create key issues that are compounded by race. We will go on to discuss certain legal and policy factors that exacerbate societal challenges from a place of governance.

Chapter 6: Law, Government and Politics

'Injustice anywhere is a threat to justice everywhere.'
– Martin Luther King Jr

In this chapter:

Challenges

- Mass incarceration and the War on Crime
- Targeted and discriminatory policing, state-sanctioned murder
- Disenfranchisement and voting
- Geopolitics and the rise of nationalism

Making things better

- Working within the system
- Increased accountability and fairer policing
- Stronger home nations and more supportive geopolitics

Our laws and how we are governed tell us much about the society we live in. They form the codes and practices that set the tone of our daily lives. They aim to give us clarity in moral direction, providing guidance on 'right' and 'wrong'. The way they have been designed to the way they are enforced tell us much about the climate and culture of the society that has been created. Laws and policies in the West have greatly impacted the reality and experience of those in the African Diaspora. From abusive policing to overt and biased sentencing and mass incarceration through to deportation measures; the picture of a 'hostile environment' for those in the Diaspora is a pretty clear one. These measures are a continuation of what was discussed previously in the Society section where we have seen policies of redlining, health disparities, and gentrification shape the way we live.

Section 1: Criminal and Punitive

Mass incarceration: a new form of slavery

Following the emancipation proclamation, a large portion of economic capital was seemingly slipping through the net of the US Treasury, creating a problematic revenue gap. The economic cost was not only felt at a national level but of course by individual slavers. However, slave owners were well-reimbursed for their lost investment but that was not the end of the financial sacrifice of enslaved people. Around £20 million was given to UK slavers as compensation for their 'lost business'; that is around £71 billion today. This sum was paid by the taxpayer up until 2015.[154] The bondage and exploitation of people is and always had been big business;

while there are many reasons why Mass incarceration has risen to prominence, a key driver is the lucrative economic opportunity provided.

The US has the highest prison population of any developed country, more than two million people incarcerated.[155] The private prison sector is a lucrative industry worth around over $9 billion, with revenues, in 2021.[156] Much like slavery, the prison-industrial complex meets the twin needs of generating large amounts of money, while also keeping people of colour in bondage. There is one key component needed to fuel the prison industrial machine—prisoners. The system is fed by hyper-targeted policing, biased criminal laws, and judicial sentencing as well as social narratives that glorify violence.

The war on drugs...war against people of colour as a means for mass incarceration

A key mechanism used to feed the machine of the mass prison system was the 'war on drugs'. This 'war' concocted by politicians seemingly to appeal to voters as being 'tough on crime', in fact, was a guise to target a specific group of people, those of colour. The strategy for the war on drugs was comprehensive, like a well-constructed political manifesto, including a media campaign to shape public perception, harassment tactics, dragnet-style search operations, financially incentivised police forces, focusing stop and search operations on particular communities, enabling the police to use 'discretion' to decide who to target, and harsh and disproportionate sentencing—all with the goal of mass incarceration.

The war on drugs began with President Nixon in 1971 but really came to life in the Reagan Era of 1982. This evolution of the war on drugs came about when the US national public opinion of the threat of drugs was less than 2%.[157]

Step 1: A Seductive Narrative to Shape Public Opinion

As with all fear-based campaigns, a scary problem needs to be created—something to rally against. We've seen this before with scaremongering campaigns around illegal immigration e.g. Brexit; in this instance, it was a drug pandemic in African American communities. The War on Drugs campaign push by President Reagan was supported by a clear and broad media narrative that painted a picture of poor Black people: ghettoised and addicted to drugs, with powerful images of crack babies and crack mothers. The face of drug use and criminality, even though drug use is largely even across different communities and in many instances higher in the White community. Interestingly, as this media narrative was being peddled in the early 1980s, crack cocaine had not even reached the ghetto community. This narrative was perpetuated despite drug use being more prevalent in the White community. A study in 2000 by the National Institute on Drug Abuse showed that White students use cocaine 7 times more than Black students and crack cocaine 8 times more than Black students and heroin 7 times more than Black students.[157]

How impactful was this media narrative in shaping the minds of the public? A study in the Journal of Alcohol and Drug Education highlighted that when a cohort of people were asked to describe a drug user, 95% pictured a Black person.[157] Yet, African Americans only constituted 15% of drug users in 1995, a similar amount to today. White people make up the majority of drug users, but they are not the stereotypical image. It is worth noting that this is not a narrative that would have been created from scratch; this was not targeting a group of people that were previously seen through a neutral lens by White America; rather this was building on a history of White supremacy, oppression and segregation. It, therefore, would not have been the biggest mental leap to create this additional negative perception of African Americans.

Step 2: Funding the Hunt

After creating a real enough threat in the public imagination, it was time to prepare for the hunt. An often-used strategy to find the true source or explanation for something is to 'follow the money'. In a world run on money, the trail of funding will usually let you know who is ultimately in charge and, in this case, what the ultimate objective was. In addition to the media frenzy, huge sums of government funding were poured into federal agencies and police departments that made the war on drugs a priority. Between 1980 and 1984, the FBI anti-drug budget jumped from $8 million to $95 million.[158] Anti-drug spending at the Department of Defence went from 33 million in 1981 to over a billion (1,042 million) in 1991.[157] In 2020, $34 billion was spent on drug enforcement, a 1090% increase in 39 years; the budget is estimated to rise to $41 billion by 2022.[159,160] The treasure chest of drug enforcement did not subside; estimates suggest that since 1971, the US government has spent over a TRILLION dollars enforcing drug policy.[159]

These huge financial injections into the combative arms of drug law enforcement were compounded with dramatic cuts to departments focused on drug treatment and prevention. The National Institute of Drug Abuse had its budget cut from $274 million to $57 million during the same period the FBI anti-drug budget ballooned (1981–1984).[157] In addition, the Department of Education budget dropped from $14 million to $3 million.[157]

The funding reached all the way down to the level of local police departments. The Byrne Program, a series of federal grants to fund local drug task forces, was begun to meet this very objective. The programme proved ineffective and costly, with limited impact on improving public safety.

Nationally, the average for narcotics spending is around 40% in all states, but in some, it was as high as 90%. In addition, in 1997, The Pentagon gave the police 1.2 million pieces of military equipment. Why do local police need so much military-grade gear to fight a war?[157]

Step 3: Executing the Hunt

The strategic and tactical execution of this war was deployed through police forces focusing their efforts primarily on poor, Black communities.

In the US, many tactics were used to arrest people of colour e.g. stop and frisk (Terry vs. Ohio, 1968), with similar stop and search also used heavily in the UK.[161,162] These policies enable law enforcement to harass any individual they deem to be suspicious, usually based on the colour of their skin. Focusing efforts on a specific community naturally leads to more arrests and convictions from that particular community.

A few policies have been enacted during the latter part of the twentieth century to help facilitate the growing prison-industrial complex with fresh blood. A key example of law enforcement with this focus was the 'broken glass' policing policies adopted in New York in the 1990s.[163] Here we saw strict policing in an attempt to set the right tone for a neighbourhood. The philosophy suggests that through tough policing of low-level crimes, people will be deterred from crime in general. This policy has yielded mixed responses with critics suggesting that even those cities that did not adopt this harsh form of policing also saw crime rates drop.

Step 4: Legal Framework to Facilitate Incarceration

In addition to the huge financial rewards attached to the war on drugs, there were many legislative introductions that helped the incarceration of people of colour. Many of these were ushered in under Democratic President Bill Clinton in the '90s with 'tough on crime' policies. Interesting to note that irrespective of the political party in power, the agenda remained the same.

This approach was broadened with the infamous 1994 Violent Crime Control and Law Enforcement Act or 1994 Crime Bill, which was passed into law with the support of President Clinton.[164,165] The charismatic, saxophone-playing President who seemed to have a good relationship with the African American community presided over one of the most devastating pieces of legislation to affect the African American community.

The Violent Crime Control and Law Enforcement Act was a lengthy crime control bill that was put together over the course of six years. Its provisions implemented many things, including a 'Three Strikes' mandatory life sentence for some repeat offenders, money to hire 100,000 new police officers, $9.7 billion in funding for prisons, and an expansion of death penalty-eligible offences. The bill also further facilitated Truth in Sentencing laws by rewarding states that required people convicted of violent crimes to serve at least 85% of their sentences. It also dedicated $6.1 billion to prevention programmes 'designed with significant input from experienced police officers'; however, the bulk of the funds were dedicated to measures that are seen as punitive rather than rehabilitative or preventative.

To cop a plea

The court system's systemic oppression continues with the use of the plea-bargaining system. If you are a hip-hop fan, there is a good chance you will have come across the phrase 'cop a plea' in one song or another. In addition to tougher sentences for low-level crimes, minimum mandatory sentences, and the 'three strikes and you're out' policy, the prominence of plea bargaining has come more to the fore in the US legal system in recent years. The idea of plea bargaining aims to get a defendant to take a deal or 'plea' for a potentially shorter sentence than they would get if they were to go to trial. In theory, you are lowering your risk of a harsher sentence by taking the sentencing deal offered by the state. This is heavily encouraged by the state as a way of processing defendants more efficiently. Usually, defendants from poorer backgrounds who are reliant on severely overworked state-provided attorneys do not have adequate legal advice to negotiate these deals properly. It is likely that they are not informed enough to even know if a good deal is being offered. These defendants often end up serving time they may not have had to, all in the name of efficiency and more importantly, to fuel the prison-industrial complex.

Disproportionate sentencing

A study shows African Americans and Latinos comprise 29% of the US population, but they make up 57% of the US prison population.[166] In some states, African Americans make up 80% to 90% of all drug offenders sent to prison.[167] In at least 15 states, African Americans are sent to prison on drug charges at a rate of 20–57 times higher than White men.[167]

Cocaine vs. crack

A key example of disproportionate sentencing that penalised African Americans was seen in the sentencing guidelines provided for those who used crack compared to those using cocaine. In the early 1990s, crack and cocaine were treated very differently in the eyes of the law despite being almost identical chemically. Crack, more commonly used by Black people at the time, was seen as 100 times more criminal than cocaine as demonstrated by the now notorious 100:1 sentencing disparity.[168] The Sentencing Commission in 1994 recommended an end to this policy, which was seen as one of the key reasons almost one in three African Americans in their 20s was either in jail, on parole, or under the purview of the criminal system.[169] However, the Republican-led

Congress at the time passed a bill to overturn the decision of the sentencing commission.

Mandatory minimums, truth in sentencing and three strikes

The might of legislation and the judiciary would be wielded against people of colour again with the introduction of mandatory minimums in the 1985 Anti-Drug Abuse Act. Mandatory minimum sentence for low level drug dealing and possession of crack cocaine of 5–10 years; in other developed countries, the standard sentence is no more than 6 months, if any jail time at all.[170] Adding further weight to legislative problems have been updates to rules like the 1998 Truth in Sentencing law, which eliminated disciplinary credits, good time, and corrections centres for certain offenders, requiring offenders to serve the entire minimum sentence prior to being considered for parole.

Closure of the courthouse

The 14th Amendment, in theory, should grant African American citizens equal and civil rights, including fair and equal treatment under the law. Of course, we have reviewed many examples of how African Americans were not receiving fair and equitable treatment in the courtroom. But who judges the judge? African Americans are stuck in an unjust system, controlled by unjust people; a system that covered its bases well under the eyes of the law. Court cases against various states, accusing them of racial discrimination in the courtroom were lost under McCleskey vs. Kemp, preventing any legal challenges of racism against prosecutors or judges.[157] This made it almost impossible to accuse or try the US legal system under any grounds of racial discrimination. The idea that if a concept is enshrined in law, it is immediately reflected in society, i.e. if it was illegal to discriminate in a courtroom—de jure prevention, then by definition, de facto (actual) racism in the courtroom would be impossible. Of course, this is not true at all, but provided a powerful counter against those who would claim racial discrimination at the hands of the law.

US Mass Incarceration, in Summary

To say that the impact of mass incarceration and the war on drugs on the Black community was HUGE is an understatement. Despite the fact the majority of illegal drug users are White, three-quarters of people imprisoned for drugs are Black or Latino—a racial bias that saw African Americans imprisoned at five times the rate of White Americans.[171] The consequences of these drug offences account for two-thirds of the rise of the federal prison population and more than half of all prisoners between 1985–2000[157]—around 500,000 prisoners in jail for drug offences today versus around 41,000 in 1980, an increase of 1,100%.[157] Drug arrests have tripled since 1980. There are more people in jail today for drug offences than for all reasons in 1980.[157] Drug trafficking occurs everywhere in the US not just in Black communities; however, Black men are admitted to state prison 13 times more often than White men.[157]

It is clear that there has been no bigger contribution to the mass incarceration of people of colour than the war on drugs.

UK Legislative Punitive Policies

While the UK isn't quite at the same advanced stage of mass incarceration and prison-industrial complexes that we see in the US, there are still policing practices used in the UK that target people of colour, for example, stop and search. In the UK, young men from Black and Minority Ethnic communities make up 44% of those in youth custody.[172] While we have not seen the same scale of legal and judicial practices that explicitly target as there is in the US, there are extensive examples of systemic and deliberate persecution of Black people in the UK.

British Policing

Stop and search

Black Brits are disproportionally impacted by the UK stop-and-search policing policy. The stop and search policy is not new but rather a reincarnation of the 'Sus' laws used to target people who looked suspicious. This type of policing while seemingly well-intentioned too often turns into harassment—harassment of anybody who fits a certain profile, typically those who belong to an ethnic minority. An argument can be made that if you are not doing anything illegal, you have nothing to worry about. Sadly, as we have seen to pronounced effect in the US, even those who are totally innocent and have nothing to hide can end up on the wrong end of a police bullet.

The Police and Criminal Evidence Act 1984 (PACE) is the legislation under which most stops and searches are currently carried out.[173] It was brought in following the repeal of a patchwork of varying powers by individual police forces to stop and search individuals including the controversial 'Sus' laws, which allowed the police to arrest someone simply for being a 'suspected person' i.e. suspicious because of your race.

According to the PACE Codes of Practice, the decision to stop and search must be based on objective information relating to a specific individual suspected of involvement in a specific offence at a specific time. In other words, that decision cannot be based on a generalised belief that a particular group of people are more likely to be involved in crime.

Looking at UK stop and search statistics in March 2020, there were 6 stop and searches for every 1,000 White people compared with 39 for every 1,000 Black people.[162] Black people are nine times as likely to be stopped and searched than White counterparts. That is clearly a huge disparity.[174] In addition, stop and search rates increased in every ethnic group except White British and Chinese (where they stayed the same). One could ask the fair question, why are the majority of minorities not being afforded the same rate of progress as the White populous? The figures show that this is clearly a long way from fair and proportional policing.

During the 2020 lockdown, around 20,000 young Black men in my city, London, were stopped and searched under excessive use of Section 60 stop and search. This is roughly a quarter of all Black men aged 15 to 24 from the capital. This is in the wake of crime rates falling in the period prior to lockdown.[175] Under section 60, no grounds for suspicion are required for the stop and search procedure; section 60 is only supposed to be used when serious violence has taken place or when there is a risk of serious violence but was clearly used excessively.

The overrepresentation of policing does not end with searching, Black people were arrested at a rate over three times higher than White people in the year ending 2020.[176]

Is this good policing?

Is this method of effective racial profiling and harassment effective? The statistics would suggest not. Only 9% of stop and searches resulted in an arrest at the peak of its use in 2008/9.[177] That proportion has increased in the years since and was 17% in 2017/18.[177] Arrests are more likely in London, with 19% of Metropolitan Police searches resulting in arrests in the same year.[177] This means that in London, 81% of stop and searches lead to no arrest, and 83% in the rest of the country.[177] Importantly, only a third of stop and searches lead to something relevant, meaning two thirds of all stop and searches are useless.[177]

Jamaican Prisons and Deportation Scandals

Another clear indicator of the position of the UK government in relation to people of Caribbean descent was the 2015 policy to spend £25 million to build a maximum-security prison in Jamaica to deport Jamaicans that were currently in British prisons.[178] The clear priority to get rid, as opposed to rehabilitate, speaks volumes. The hostile environment that was championed by former Prime Minister Theresa May was seen again with the 'Go Home' anti-immigration vans.

Deporting Caribbean Brits

This policy was continued in 2020 with another large Jamaican deportation scandal.[179] After decades of living and working in Britain, many members of the Windrush generation were wrongly classified as illegal immigrants and treated horrifically. This occurred solely because they arrived as children with their invited parents, so at the time of arrival did not have their own passports. In several cases, these individuals had families here and, in some cases, no real ties to Jamaica. Moreover, similar situations have arisen for Nigerians and Ghanaians. This scandal was the result of Theresa May and the UK conservative government's 'Hostile Environment' initiative aimed at making the UK unliveable for any undocumented immigrant. People who had spent all their lives living in the UK, contributing to society, and paying tax were subject to oppressive treatment, including being taken to detention centres and perhaps worse, actually deported. Six months later, the government apologised and promised to redress those wrongs and pay compensation. More than 2,000 people have now had their citizenship formally recognised by the government.[180] The idea that Black Caribbeans who had spent the majority of their lives living and working in the UK, contributing to the country—many of whom were part of rebuilding the country following World War II—would now be deported like criminals is a pretty big indictment of the UK political system, and sends a pretty clear message about how the establishment views this group.

State-Sanctioned Murder – The Long Arm of the Law

As if racial profiling and targeting from law enforcement wasn't enough, we have seen recorded evidence all too often of live executions of people of colour at the hands of officers of the law. This has been going on since slavery has been brought to the attention of the global population through the advent of camera phones and social media. The murder of Black people at the hands of White people has gone frequently without punishment. This is unsurprising given the historic dynamic between the two groups in the West was one of property and owner.

Moving forward through the sands of time: through reconstruction, the formation of the KKK, and into the civil rights era to the late twentieth century and up to the present day, what we see is a transition of the terror campaigns of the KKK through to the state-sponsored execution at the hands of police officers.

It is worth pausing for a moment and reflecting on the multiple deaths that were caught on camera from Rodney King in the early '90s, Tamir Rice, Eric Garner, Mike Brown, Fidel Castro, Trayvon Martin, Sandra Bland, to George Floyd and numerous others who were not caught on camera (the prospect of the true number is frightening).

This is not unique to the US. This is a global problem for people across the Diaspora. We see the persecution faced by Black people in South America, in particular Brazil and Colombia. Black people form the majority of the poorest people in these countries and are often targeted by the police.

In the UK, the same campaign of terror is perpetuated, though not to the same extent, I suspect largely because of the fact that ordinary officers do not carry firearms. We have seen the figures for how the UK police target people of colour, so the extrapolation of how these interactions would end if firearms were available is a small leap. Even without the presence of firearms, we still see people of colour in the UK die in police custody. Black people account for 3% of the population in the UK but make up 8% of those who die in police custody.[181]

In Brazil, a country with the largest Diaspora representation at about 56 million people,[182] Afro or Black Brazilians suffer terribly from police brutality. It has been reported that every 23 minutes, a young Afro-Brazilian is killed.[183] Afro-Brazilians make up about 55% of the population; they were 75% of those killed by the police in 2017 and 2018.[183]

Tragic enough

In 2020, we saw the rise of the Black Lives Matter (BLM) movement in response to multiple executions on US soil, in particular Ahmaud Arbery and George Floyd. The death of George Floyd was particularly significant in drawing global attention to ongoing racial injustice. The 46-year-old man was choked to death by the knee of police officer Derek Chauvin live on camera. The grotesque murder took 8 minutes and 42 seconds. Slowly but surely, second by second, George's life was taken away. A few things stand out about this death: the time taken for the execution to take place and the cool head of the four officers involved in the murder, who ignored the protests of the members of the public who filmed the crime and pleaded with the officers to stop. The calmness of the officer committing murder clearly demonstrated the confidence he had in a system that would protect him, despite there being live footage.

As we know, the death of Black people at the hands of the police is nothing new, neither is the video footage. However, this led to a global backlash like never before—protests in 50 states and over 50 countries worldwide, public condemnation and support from the business. Why did this get such a big response compared to all the previous filmed murders? I think a combination of factors set this murder apart, but in particular, it was the length of time and the method of execution. Watching the lengthy video is enough to touch even the coldest of hearts. The slow method deployed of neck on throat, crushing the life out of the cuffed, unarmed man as he called out for his mother was a whole new level of brutal. Now, this is not to put his death on a higher pedestal than anybody else's, but rather just to note that people have already become desensitised to muffled gunfire from a few shots that are usually used to kill African Americans.

What Drives the Police Murder of Unarmed Black People?

I have often wondered what the motivation for these continued killings is. You would hope that there is, on some level, a common feeling of humanity that makes it difficult for one person to kill another. We know there are many examples of soldiers who have struggled to take another's life at war, so how do we get to a place where this humanity is lost? I believe the answer lies in the exact way some people, in this instance law enforcement, have been historically cultivated to view Black people; a deep penetrating dehumanisation that makes pulling the trigger significantly easier because, after all, we are perceived as less than. The roots of this originate from slavery and have been seemingly carefully preserved to the present day.

This abhorrent view of inferiority must be culturally endemic in the force insidiously permeating all aspects from police training, though to stop and searches, harassment, profiling, and the rest. In the UK, Black males fall under the code 'IC3'. Of course, there are codes for lots of different groups, but I can't help but wonder what psychological conscious and subconscious triggers are activated when that code comes across the radio…immediately a heightened sense of alertness, aggressiveness, and training that says these people need to be handled harshly and knowledge that, by and large, you will be protected from retribution, regardless how you treat them. This sadly is not speculation or hyperbole, it's present-day reality—In April 2022, in the US, a Michigan police chief issued a public apology after reports that images of Black men were used as targets in the department's training area.

Like the entirety of this book examining different examples of discrimination, injustice, and oppression across practically all aspects of life, there is ample evidence to back up the rotten culture within the policing profession, not just the numerous incidents of harassment, abuse, and murder, but also official independent reviews into policing. On February 1, 2022, the Independent Office for Police Conduct (IPOC) released findings from the Operation Hotton Investigation. The damning report identified cultural and systemic issues of racism and misogyny.[184]

There are likely loftier, external motives also at play that encourage and facilitate the abusive treatment of Black people by law enforcement. A convenient and distracting political football is created when a Black person is murdered, which provides the average working-class White person with a subject to feel superior to; after all, at least they don't have to worry about that level of brutality—'there is inherent value in being White, even if I have little else'. Despite all that we have seen with the relationship between law enforcement and Black people, it's worth remembering it is all learned behaviour and as such, in theory, can be unpicked, unlearned and dismantled.

The Right Way to Protest

Following the death of every Black person at the hands of the police, a similar pattern forms, one now of social media shock, outrage and hashtags, pain of the respective family and community, negatively biased media coverage that tries to discredit the victim, a police press conference defending the officer, faces on t-shirts, and then a *protest*. George Floyd's death led to global protests, protests that were occasionally co-opted by other groups like ANTIFA, and at times led to small spates of damage that became front and centre of biased media coverage. However, in reality, the protests were mainly peaceful.

In January 2021, White Trump supporters stormed the US Capitol, fighting with police, breaking windows and forcing entry into the building. Significant damage was caused to the building, rioters stood on the desks of officials and generally ran amuck. The police response was soft, with some officers choosing to take selfies with rioters. Despite all the damage and violence, only a few people were arrested and, of course, nobody was killed. We need to take a moment to recognise that this riot took place within the heart of Western democracy. It was domestic terrorism, yet no misplaced shots were fired; miraculously, officers were not fearing for their lives despite being physically assaulted. The world saw a very restrained and understanding police force, one that seemed to not even be able to consider violent action, not even self-defence. The response of law enforcement was so tepid, it could almost be considered complicit. If the world ever needed a demonstration of the disparity in treatment between White and Black people, this was it. This contrast is made even more stark when compared to the peaceful BLM protest in the US Capitol a couple of years before, which was met with dozens of storm-trooper-style armed guards, seemingly poised to quickly and lethally put down any hint of unrest—two completely different worlds somehow occupying the same reality.

Section 2: Beyond the Criminal

As discussed, governments targeting people of colour are not limited to being punitive. Barriers are also seen in other areas of government policy; for example, disenfranchisement and the growing political right-wing/nationalist movements we see around the world.

Disenfranchisement and Voting

A major consequence of life after prison is the effective second-class citizen status you inherit. The 2020 US elections have shown that not everyone is afforded the opportunity to express their democratic right to vote. History and present-day feedback would suggest not. America, the supposed land of the free, has a big problem with voter suppression—barriers put in place that prevent or inhibit people from voting. These tactics are often used to stifle the African American vote. A meme recently showed a real picture of a White female astronaut casting her vote via satellite phone from space, with the caption highlighting that it is easier for a White woman to vote from space than an African American in America. This is obviously a facetious example, but the facts on the ground show you there is no smoke without fire.

Historic examples of voter suppression of African Americans include poll taxes (prohibitive fees to vote) and literacy tests (IQ tests to determine if one should be given their constitutional right to vote). The 1965 Voting Rights Act, an important milestone of the civil rights movement, blunted many of these racist tools, in part by requiring places with a history of voting discrimination (e.g. Texas) to get voting changes cleared at a federal level before they become state law.[185] However, in 2013, the US Supreme Court removed this law, freeing states from federal oversight and unleashing a wave of new voting restrictions, including new voter ID laws and efforts to close polling locations.[186]

Let's take a look at some of the present-day suppressive tactics:

Going postal

Texas is a Republican stronghold, with a growing minority population that threatens to turn it blue (Democratic state). In the 2020 election, Texas only allowed mail-in votes if voters were 65 or older or met certain other conditions.[187] The state does not allow people to register to vote online, forcing you to register in person. These may seem like small things, but they have an impact; and remember this is voting—a core constitutional and democratic right. All this during a pandemic when it would be most sensible to facilitate remote voting.

Texas Governor Greg Abbott, a Republican, has issued an order that will limit each county to one mail drop box.[188] The move means that Democratic-friendly Harris County, which covers more than 1,700 square miles and is home to 2.4 million registered voters, can only offer one place for voters to return their ballots.

Mail delay concerns

With huge backlogs caused by Covid, Democrats were concerned that some votes would be late. Now, you may think a late vote, as long as it was cast before the November 3 deadline would be okay. No such luck. The Republicans pushed for states to only count votes that are counted by election day. The Pennsylvania Supreme Court has ordered a three-day extension, but courts in Michigan and Wisconsin, two key swing states have decided to stick with the November 3 deadline.[189] In 2016, Trump only won Michigan by 10,000 votes and Wisconsin by under 23,000.

Can I get a witness?

Some states not only require a signature from the voter but also that of a witness. This is clearly an additional hurdle that makes casting your vote harder. Some ballots have already been thrown out because this requirement was not met.[190]

Secret envelopes

As if there weren't enough barriers, there is also a rule in some states of a 'secrecy envelope'. This is where a second envelope is needed to cover the first known as the 'naked ballot'. States with this policy will not count naked ballots. Democrats have argued against this, stating that discarding naked ballots violated the right to have one's vote counted. Pennsylvania's Supreme Court decided to keep the secrecy envelope requirement in place.[191]

Ten-hour waits

In Georgia, thousands of voters waited hours just to cast their ballot during early voting. Many attribute the long wait to voter enthusiasm, but other factors like a limited number of polls, understaffing, or computer glitches have also been blamed.[192]

Prison bans

Many US states restrict the voting rights of convicts. Some states automatically restore voting rights after the sentence is served, while others wait until after probation and parole are served, and after all fines have been paid. In 2018, Florida restored the voting rights of 1.5 million non-violent felons. Soon after, the state amended the law to say that felons must prove they have paid all fines and fees before they vote.[193] Supreme Court Justice, Sonia Sotomayor said the move would block people from voting 'simply because they are poor'. An estimated 774,000 people in Florida, one of the closest swing states in the country, can't vote because they owe money.[193]

The risk of voter suppression was extended in 2021 in the state of Georgia, which passed voting laws (18–13) that would again limit voting access to African Americans. The new laws will require ID for mail-in ballots, prevent unofficial workers from handing out food in voting lines and limit the number of drop boxes for absentee votes, meaning people will have to travel further to vote.[194] On the surface, these laws that are positioned to make voting more secure clearly make the practice more challenging for African Americans and other minorities.

Government Education Policies Barriers to Higher Education – EMA Removal

Away from restrictions to voting, we see other examples of government interventions that disproportionately, and negatively, impact people of colour.[195] A challenge with some discriminatory policies is that they are more discreet and subtle in their execution than more traditional forms. These usually take the guise of cuts to public funding that disproportionately affect those who are worst off and by proxy those from minority backgrounds.

A good example of this was the UK Conservative policy to cut the 'Education Maintenance Allowance' (EMA) programme. This small weekly subsidy was created to support those from low-income families who wanted to study for their A-Levels or study at the college level. I personally fell into this category of a lower-income student who benefited from this weekly fund, enabling me to study without having to work, a choice that many people are forced to make. Cutting this allowance has added a further boundary to those who already have had to face challenges to make it to this level of education, which is a critical gateway to higher education and studying at university.

Higher Tuition Fees

Another example of a prohibitive policy deterring poorer people from accessing higher education was the rise in tuition fees. The trebling of fees to £9,000 a year meant that students wanting to study for a degree had to face the dilemma of being saddled with a large amount of debt if they were to pursue this course.[196] The intersection of race and class coming into effect again here with the near privatisation of education, selectively preventing poorer students from accessing an important tool for social mobility. A degree isn't the guarantee to a great career, but it is a solid foundation and is usually essential for more technical vocations such as an architect or doctor.

Geo-Politics – Weak Global Perception and Lack of International Support

I would like to briefly make note of the broader, international position; we see that there are large disparities of power and influence on a geo-political level. With clear ties cut between the Diaspora and mother countries in Africa, and the general economic and political weakness of African and Caribbean nations, there is no possibility for international pressure from these countries to be exerted on Western nations that have become home to people of colour. If we think about other ethnic groups who have clearer connections to their home country, e.g. people from India, Pakistan or perhaps Chinese people or those from the Middle East, countries that are also economically, militarily and politically more advanced than African and Caribbean countries; it is clear to see that the US and other Western powers would perhaps think more carefully before treating them with the same disregard Black people are subject to. I think what is particularly interesting is people from Middle Eastern countries. We have spent the best part of 20 years in a 'War on Terror' that has led to a lot of deplorable Islamophobic behaviour; yet while Islamic people have taken the brunt of Western resentment, we do not see Muslims being murdered in the street to anywhere near the same extent.

Moreover, we see many stories of people from the Diaspora treated badly in foreign countries and not only those in the West. In 2020 following the outbreak of COVID-19, many Africans were evicted from apartments and hotels in Guangzhou, China. Guangzhou is a hub for African traders and home to one of China's largest African communities. A branch of McDonald's in Guangzhou also refused to serve Black people. It feels like something from apartheid South Africa or segregated America, but this was in 2020.[197]

Even more recently in 2022, following the Russian invasion of Ukraine, Africans based in Ukraine trying to flee like everyone else were prevented from boarding trains leaving the country and denied access to shelter in neighbouring countries like Poland. Many of these Africans were students (Africans make up 20% of Ukraine's foreign student body).[198] This was another stark example of the harsh treatment people in the Diaspora were subjected to knowing there is no risk of retribution from weak African nations.

With parents who are both Jamaican and Ghanaian, I've spent time in these countries over the past couple of decades and seen the progress that is being made. However, there is still a long way to go before they will hold international weight; and much of their development is dependent on foreign investment from the West and China, making them less likely to try and challenge the treatment of people of colour abroad and risk their financial funding.

The weakness of our home nations is further exacerbated by debt colonialism: the economic weight that most African countries are still under following liberation. This debt imposed by former colonial rulers is implemented in different ways, from a direct sum as severance from the colony to structured loans with high-interest rates or forms of 'tide aide' where an amount is loaned to a country, but that money has to be used to buy goods from the donating country. It has also been suggested that political influence has been given in exchange for funds. In 2019, more than 30 African countries paid more in debt than they did on public healthcare.[199] The debt programmes (Structural Adjustment Policies SAPs) of the '80s and '90s are widely acknowledged to have led to decades of under-investment in public services. Part of the condition of the SAPs was an economic restructuring that determined where national funds were spent, typically on servicing debt and not on public services or initiatives. The subsequent neglect of public services prevented countries from developing the human and social capital needed to repay the debt in the first place.[199] Furthermore, financial Western powerhouses, the IMF and World Bank, demanded that developing countries had to lower their standard of living to pay their debts.

Unfortunately, many African countries were not given much hope for success from independence in the '60s. The weak foundations left and encouraged by colonial powers were not what was needed for burgeoning nations. Economic policies, such as high export dependence, concentrated on only a few commodities that were also being provided by other developing nations, led to a race to the bottom in terms of low pricing and unfavourable trade terms: severely devaluing local resources to the benefit of the West and developed world. Countries have also been advised to devalue their currencies in order to help with debt repayment.

Furthermore, to attract foreign investment, regulations for international companies were minimised and penalisation for foreign companies leaving the country was removed, increasing the risk of 'capital flight' (the removal of investment) at any given time, and creating instability and uncertainty. The engineered race to the bottom meant that countries invested less domestically in their own industries and created fewer local business-to-business and business-to-consumer dynamics, which decreased the multiplier effect of circulating domestic revenue i.e. the amount of money that could benefit multiple groups of people. These policies were promoted and supported by the Paris Club (a collective of representatives from wealthy nations), IMF, and World Bank with devastating impact on the developing African economies.[200] In addition to all of these external challenges, internal corruption and financial mismanagement made a difficult situation even worse.

Political: Future State – The Rise of Nationalism

At the start of the book, I discussed the 'problem' of 'what to do with these people?' that the respective Western elites had to deal with following the breakdown of the slave trade, entering the post-colonial era and following post-World War II reconstruction (with respect to the UK specifically). Millions of people needed a new purpose for being residents in countries where the primary objective was servitude had now outstayed their welcome.

In the latter part of the last decade (2016–2022), we have seen a steady rise in nationalism and far-right rhetoric, most aptly captured in the UK Brexit result, its surrounding narratives, and the election of President Trump in the US, on a ticket of 'Make America Great Again'. We are in a time where the reverberations of the 2008/9 economic crash are still being felt through the strain of austerity and where an increasingly globalised and technologically driven business world is making the Western working-class masses feel increasingly obsolete.

The combination of low establishment valuation, because of lack of current service beyond the public sectors; mixed with growing xenophobia and rising nationalism, driven by scarcity of resource among the working classes, puts the Diaspora in a particularly vulnerable position, subject to attack from all sides. The Diaspora are subject to a combination of top-down pressure from the ruling elite in the shape of the discriminatory policy change and decreased funding of public services in addition to misplaced bottom-up pressure from the disgruntled White working class. The result of these converging waves is a 'hostile environment' for those in the Diaspora who, for most, will continue to sit at the bottom of the societal food chain.

I would like to again acknowledge the intersection between race and class, which is somewhat inherent with the majority of the Diaspora residing in poorer and working-class strata of society. Many of the socioeconomic problems faced by people within the same socioeconomic background are the same irrespective of race, e.g. underfunded schools, poorer healthcare, and a more dangerous living environment.

In a common strategy executed by those in power, 'divide and conquer' tactics are employed to keep different factions of the most vulnerable parts of society fighting against each other. Resulting in the far-right/alt-right pitting themselves against different ethnic minorities who are facing the same social struggles, but have been cleverly misdirected to focus on topics of immigration as the root cause of their issues as opposed to, say, fairer distribution of wealth.

While challenges can be common, and it is reductive to get into a contest of who suffers more in a vulnerable community, it shows that there is a greater disadvantage to being a person of colour.

The 'racial bribe' following Bacon's revolt in 1676 was a great example of social elites playing strategic divide and conquer, where poor White farmers were offered privileges and preferential status over their Black peers to build a wedge between the two working-class groups.[201] This divide prevented the two groups from partnering against a common elitist enemy and instead pitted them against one another along racial lines. This divide has been perpetuated throughout time with the vast majority of far-right members coming from the poorer parts of society, seeing those of colour or foreign origin as their main enemy positioned as competition for jobs and public sector resources e.g. school places and hospital beds—convenient distractions from those at the top of the pyramid who continue to get richer and control the show.

Making Things Better

Accountable policing, better policing practices and Defunding

There is an officer behind the trigger of each gun used to kill a Black person. Holding individual officers more accountable for their actions would go a long way toward decreasing the number of police murders. If officers genuinely face the threat of jail time, losing their job, or serious financial punishments—as a normal citizen would—they would think more carefully before pulling the trigger. Remove qualified immunity. Increase accountability. Go after individual pensions.

It is a known fact that there is a culture of collective protection within the force. This brotherhood helps to facilitate the crimes; it is also something that needs to be tackled. How are officers being trained? Are they being psychologically screened well enough? Do higher bars of education and empathy need to be introduced? These are all valid questions for people who are given the responsibility to protect but the power to kill—largely without consequence.

Finally, the concept of defunding the police or redistributing financial resources has been suggested as a solution. The redistribution would mean fewer officers and more resources for community and crime prevention programmes; this too could be an effective deterrent for police killings while freeing up funds to improve communities in other ways.

De-escalation...with Black people too

In October 2021, 27-year-old Walter Wallace Jr was shot ten times and killed by officers, after he was acting erratically with a knife. The officers asked Walter to put the knife down, but he did not respond. The officers pursued him in an effort to disarm him for about a minute before shots were fired. His mum, and other neighbours also in the area, witnessed his death. Wallace, a father of seven suffered from mental health issues and was on medication. In this instance, there was a clear need for de-escalation. Without trivialising the level of threat posed by Wallace, there is likely to be some threat level during police work, and murder should be the last resort in any instance. We also know from many examples of dangerous White suspects that end with peaceful arrests that when desired, the police can choose to restrain from lethal force—so the issue is clearly race.

Here are some examples of de-escalation that could also be used with Black people to help preserve life:

- Warning shots—A knife vs. a gun, most people know who is winning, so while Wallace appeared to be approaching the officers, there was no attempt to fire a warning shot to get him to back off safely.
- Taser—A taser could have been used to safely incapacitate him.

- Shots to incapacitate and not kill—This is harder to execute, but they could have shot at his legs/feet; there would have been a minimal chance of a fatal wound and he would have been incapacitated.
- Mental health de-escalation—Wallace's mum was present and made it clear that her son had mental health problems. Are police trained to manage threats from people who are mentally ill? No tactics were employed to address someone who is mentally ill.

As we know too well, Walter's story is not an isolated instance, and too often no attempt is made to safely de-escalate a situation before resorting to lethal force. In comparison, we have seen many White people pose a significant danger to the public, threaten and assault police officers and still live to tell the tale. From Bryan Riley, who killed a baby, mother, and grandmother before shooting at police to the massacre of Dylann Roof, so many White perpetrators have been arrested without loss of life.[202]

Activism and systemic change (operating within the system)

Broadly speaking, both the left and right in the US and UK are working within similar political frameworks. They offer different flavours of the same concept, with the most preferential spin for people of colour often from what's on offer by the left. This is usually because the left caters better to those on the lower rungs of society, which is where the majority of Black people reside. However, if we look for any concrete policies Democratic President Obama specifically provided African Americans, you would be searching for a long time, though it must be acknowledged that Obamacare, the more universal healthcare offering, did benefit poorer African Americans and others. We have already spoken about some of the devastating policies that were ushered in under the Clinton Presidency.

Without a revolution and total upheaval of the current political system, we are forced to operate within it. I don't know what a drastically different system would look like, so while that is being worked out, we need to do the best we can with what we have and look to function within it.

Change can be a slow process, especially systemic change. However, we have seen and reaped the benefits of political activism and change. The entire civil rights movements on both sides of the pond were directly responsible for many of the liberties we benefit from today, from the UK Bristol Bus Boycott to the US Birmingham movement.[203,204] The system is not perfect, but as of today we have to operate within it, and that requires participation.

We have to be politically aware of the policies different parties are putting forward and the impact they will have on the community. The more organised and present the political group, the more political parties are willing to create policies that benefit that group. In addition, we need more MPs, governors, senators and lords from the Diaspora who are willing to advocate on behalf of the people. David Lammy to Diane Abbott, Bernie Grant and Charlotta A. Bass to Barack Obama… these representatives are important. Again, these public servants will not be perfect; they too are operating within the same system, but it is currently what we have to work with.

Legislation/systems overall?

It is necessary to have the legal system on your side, imperative almost. Despite law often being used against people of colour, it can be used to defend our civil liberties and freedoms, and after all, that is how this society is supposed to function—protection under the law, despite how fanciful that may sound given the current societal realities we live in.

Addressing voting barriers

We have seen that voting isn't so easy in the US, and sadly, a lot of these barriers will impact African Americans. Any policy that may bar people from their democratic right to vote should be examined carefully and challenged. A key way to fight this disenfranchisement would be democratically through voting and policy change, but there are barriers here too. Historically, African Americans were not allowed to vote. Even as free people, it wasn't until the middle of the twentieth century that this was legally overturned.

During the Jim Crow era, there were many barriers preventing African Americans from exercising their democratic right to vote: voting fees or poll taxes that prevented the majority of the poor African Americans from voting, literacy tests that prevented many illiterate African Americans from voting, grandfather clauses that stopped African Americans from voting based on their slave ancestry. The disenfranchisement barriers have continued through into the modern 'New Jim Crow' era. Those who have felon status, which is practically anyone who has had contact with the criminal justice system from plea bargaining upwards, have forfeited their right to vote and many other civic liberties such as welfare support.

Addressing voting barriers is particularly important because the disenfranchisement of African Americans curtails their voting numbers and subsequently their political bargaining weight with Democrats and Republicans. With less political collateral to bargain with it is even harder to demand or negotiate policy change that will benefit the community.

More tolerant political narratives

The entire world can benefit from more tolerant and less polarising political narratives. Because of huge wealth disparities, increasing pressures on public services, and rising unemployment, we see a move to more polarising narratives that seek to provide easy answers to relatively complex political problems of economy, employment, and immigration. Political narratives that promote tolerance, acceptance and not blaming those most vulnerable in society will help. Trump-style politics that embolden racists and promote violence like the invasion of the Capitol and the Charlottesville protests, where Heather Heyer was killed by a car, are not what is needed in a civilised society.[205,206]

Reformative and rehabilitative prison systems – Nordic systems

Changing the prison system from a business that profits from the lives of incarcerated individuals to a system that focuses on the rehabilitation of citizens into productive members of society is vital.[207] I'm not naïve enough to think that this is possible for every person. There are some people who cannot be 'saved' as such, but I do believe the intention behind the objective of the system counts for a lot, and if that objective is to get as many people to serve the maximum amount of time in the pursuit of profit, then something is wrong. If we look at the prison system in Scandinavian countries, we see a totally different approach is taken, which yields much better results. Less reoffending and ex-prisoners that are better set up to contribute to society—surely that should be the goal.

International weakness/geopolitics

With the challenges facing the Diaspora around the globe, where can we turn to for help? The sad truth is that African and Caribbean countries are not yet strong enough to lend much international support. There is the logistical issue of tracing your heritage back to a country, in some cases e.g. African heritage prior to displacement the Caribbean, but even if that obstacle was surmountable, the African nations are not strong enough to lend help. You can imagine a scenario where the targeting and persecution of people of the African Diaspora were challenged with a phone call from the president of Ghana or Nigeria to the White House. One day hopefully, African nations will be in a position to give international political support. This idea should not seem too far-fetched. For centuries now, countries all over the world have gladly extracted African wealth and resources, from diamonds to coltan and cobalt. If these resources were under more domestic control, they would be powerful bargaining chips and, obviously, valuable national resources that could serve the countries they belong to but that is a different discussion.

The Interconnectedness of Law and Government

We see the challenges of law, government, and politics, particularly around mass incarceration, the prison-industrial complex and police brutality connect well with narratives of dangerous Black men and angry Black women that are spread in the media. They are complementarily tied to the promotion of violent music and culture that catalyse the production of potential offenders and a dehumanised view of Black people. Moreover, as touched upon earlier, issues of redlining and underfunded neighbourhoods, poorer-performing schools, and high exclusion rates create an ideal environment for overt, targeted policing and the fostering of the prison pipeline. We also see that discriminatory policies that impede voting are from the same family of discriminatory policies that prevented access to federal housing benefits. Finally, government policies that unfairly impact those with lower incomes that are largely Black, like the removal of initiatives like the Education Maintenance Allowance (EMA) or increased tuition fees, add barriers to social mobility.

Chapter 7: Narratives, Media, Music and Entertainment

'Rhythm and blues used to be called race music...this music was going on for years, but nobody paid any attention to it.'
– Ray Charles

In this chapter:

Challenges

- Negative narratives and images
- Under-representation and misrepresentation in the media
- The Western beauty standard

Making things better

- Creating our own narratives
- Increasing knowledge of self
- Broader representation and more balanced consumption of information

Negative Narratives and Images

Our image or self-perception is often communicated through the narratives, the stories we tell ourselves and each other. As humans, we are dependent on stories to communicate, learn and socialise. Stories are at the heart of how we form our beliefs and share knowledge. As such, they can be extremely powerful tools of control and can be key to shaping our realities. We have seen the power of narratives throughout history and what they enable people to do, think, and feel.

People will literally give their lives for what they believe. These beliefs are just a set of ideas that form a narrative or story: religious allegories that shape the lives of billions to the social contracts and currency fables we tell each other every day to keep the world spinning—why one piece of paper representing a certain amount can be exchanged for a sandwich—to the darker narratives and propaganda machine of fascist regimes that led to millions of deaths during the Holocaust, millions of deaths during the communist era, and millions of deaths during transatlantic slavery, through to the current situation of people in the African Diaspora.

Narratives and stories are so powerful that when wielded correctly they can become more like spells, and those in control become more like wizards. For a contemporary view of this, just recall the furore and emotional impact generated during the Brexit Leave campaign, especially around issues of immigration. The story of endless streams of immigrants descending on the UK to steal jobs and resources, despite evidence of immigration being extremely beneficial to the country.

Similarly, in the US with the Make America Great Again narrative, the story focused on bringing America back to a mid-twentieth century 'paradise' when milkshakes were thick, burgers fat, and people of darker complexion knew their place. This story too played on the fears of the immigration narrative and was implemented to great effect. Instead of the accurate communication of the real problems with the American economy like why a once successful car industry was dying—because jobs were sacrificed in the name of globalisation, capitalism and profit—was magically repositioned as an issue of immigration to great effect.

A frightening part of our narrative-led behaviour is that our stories do not have to make any sense; there does not need to be any logic to what we say and therefore, believe. For example, going into World War II in the 1930s, African Americans were leaving behind a country that was steeped in segregation and oppression, a country where they were effectively second-class citizens. These Americans were told to go and fight a global threat in Europe that stood against freedom, a freedom that they were not afforded in their own home country—a completely paradoxical argument. This huge level of hypocrisy was not a problem for White Americans, African Americans were expected to accept it.

What comes to mind with the narratives of the modern-day members of the African Diaspora? What is the common perception? Is it one of educational excellence or business prowess? A vision of spiritual serenity? Or is it something else? The narrative that has been perpetuated consistently of the African American or Black Brit is one of entertainment at best and villain at worst, the ultra-dangerous, super predator of Hillary Clinton's '90s' imagination.[208] Quite often, the two are combined. This is particularly surprising when we take into account some of the significant contributions made by members of the Diaspora from the great inventors mentioned earlier to writers such as Maya Angelou or Garrett Morgan. Often, these names are kept in obscurity, like the nose shot off the Sphinx in Egypt to prevent true history from being shown. This is the name of the game: control the narrative and subsequently control what people believe.

Despite the systemic struggles placed on the people of the Diaspora, we have seen innovation and progress. These stories are rarely championed; instead, what we more commonly see as the typical representation of members of the Diaspora in mainstream media from music to magazines is one of entertainer—musician, athlete, or actor.

Why is the image of a Gangster Rapper more favourable than that of a Conscious Rapper? Why is the image of an athlete promoted more than that of a scholar? The negative stereotypes are implicit in maintaining a cycle that began with the sub-human classification that justified slavery and persists today to exonerate mass incarceration and police brutality. Notions of Black kids being labelled as troublesome in primary school years continue along with the fast track to placement in educational groups for lower attainment and then achieving lower grades in secondary education grades or worse yet exclusion before even being able to sit exams.

This cycle is key to facilitating and feeding other aspects of the network. It's fundamental to the future pipeline of prison candidates and low-level achievers, for the younger generations to feel compelled to aspire to a glamorous but dangerous lifestyle. Positioned as 'cool', 'tough', or 'dangerous', the image of negativity is paramount.

Toxic Narratives/Stereotypes

Here are a handful of unhealthy and negative narratives that have been perpetuated about the Black community.

Toxic masculinity/hypermasculinity

Toxic masculinity is a psychological phenomenon widely encouraged and perpetuated in Black men. Hillary Clinton in 1996 coined the term 'super predator' as a broad descriptor of Black men with 'no conscience'.[208] The idea of the criminal or threatening Black man is a prevailing one and one that is pushed at a frighteningly early age. This narrative is something that is important in the process of dehumanising individuals. If Black men are all violent animals, it is much easier to condone police brutality, mass incarceration and racism in general.

Stemming from negative narratives of being a thug or gangster, the idea that the Black man has to be emotionless and aggressively masculine at all times is something that will have an impact on Black men, the Black community and broader society. In reality, all people vary; some people naturally conform to more masculine stereotypes, whilst others are more emotional. What happens if you don't feel like you can express yourself? What happens after a day of subjugation and discrimination, and you don't feel like you can show weakness? This obviously isn't healthy, particularly for someone's mental state. This mindset to some degree has hangovers from slavery—a time where both men and women were forced to be physically strong and were brutalised into becoming more beast than man. We all feel and express different emotions; no one person is just one thing all the time.

Stifling parts of your personality or nature or being prevented from expressing it is going to have unhealthy repercussions.

Women with attitude/'strong' Black woman

An equally unhealthy but sadly common stereotype is one of the 'strong' Black woman, someone who can withstand all the stresses and pressures of an unfair world while remaining controlled and handling her business and that of her family. While this is a very true stereotype that should be celebrated, there is also a more damaging side. The negative consequence of the mentality is the lack of scope for being able to show weakness and fragility, something, as discussed in the male example, that is unavoidably human. We are not robots; we all need time and opportunity to show our softer side. This perception again can be used perversely to justify harsher treatment toward this demographic. This is something observed during years of slavery when medical experiments were performed on African American women without anaesthetic to today where we see the frequent omission from popular culture.

'Aggressive'

An equally toxic trope is the idea of Black women and men being inherently aggressive. I think there is a connection here to women who are assertive in general, in that they are being seen to overstep their current 'societal bounds' and displaying what may be seen as more 'masculine confidence'. This is often the misinterpretation when in actual fact they are just being. Perhaps they are showing an opinion and being confident enough and robust enough to defend that opinion. I think of the Misha B incident from the 2011 season of the UK show *The X Factor*. Misha was accused of being mean to other contestants, de facto bullying, by two of the judges live on the show. Misha, then 19, strongly refuted these claims, and later said the treatment she received on the show made her suicidal.[209] How can a 19-year-old be accused of bullying while she was being bullied? A teenager, like anyone else, has her flaws, but the easy go-to narrative was one of bully and aggressor, an all-too-familiar story for Black women.

'Bad bitches'

The narrative of the Bad Bitch is one that is amplified in mainstream music with the likes of Megan Thee Stallion, Stefflon Don, Doja Cat, and Nicki Minaj, to name a few. The hypersexualised Black woman is, however, not a new concept; this narrative was used by White slave owners as an excuse to rape female enslaved people. The exploitation in contemporary times is slightly more subtle. Of course, as we know the record label and media outlet owners are by and large White, these are the people ultimately benefiting from the salacious personas projected and created for these Black women. There is an argument to say that women in general are exploited sexually and this is a manifestation of the patriarchy, but this seems to be disproportionately stacked when it comes to women of colour. Songs like *Wet Ass Pussy (W.A.P)* are overtly sexual and would not be performed by the likes of Taylor Swift, who is the approximate equivalent in terms of popularity among the White community.

This narrative, like the other negative narratives communicated about the Black community, serves to dehumanise and devalue us. If Black women are portrayed as promiscuous, it's easier to turn a blind eye when they go missing or not report on it at all; it's easier to feel disconnected when a Black woman is brutalised or killed by law enforcement. The effects can also be even more insidiously pervasive, infiltrating the mentality of future generations. When young Black boys and girls grow up watching these images and internalising these concepts, we see the girls gravitating towards ideals that lead to less self-respect and the boys growing to view women as people who should not be honoured—leading to a shaky foundation for future families and households.

'Bad-ass kids'

The unfair assertions and negative tropes do not stop with adults but actually start in childhood. Often, we see young children, especially boys, unfairly branded as troublemakers early on. This is a major problem as it is readily incorporated into the fabric of school systems and seen with teachers being on high alert with Black students from an early age, an unconscious bias with damaging consequences. As discussed earlier, I have first-hand experience of negative encounters with primary and secondary school teachers who on reflection were unnecessarily hypervigilant with me in comparison to other kids. I've reflected on the heightened level of attention my wrongdoings were given compared to other students. As the only Black child in the class, I can only presume this was because of my race. Sadly, we see this played out in the propensity for exclusion and often patronising behaviour with parents and lower expectations for the children.

Aside from the unfair assertion that all people from one demographic could only be these negative archetypes, there are broader additional impacts of these perpetuated views. In a world that continues to become more divisive and increasingly more segregated, where fewer people engage with one another through a perspective of understanding and compassion, viewing people through a negative lens constructed under false pretences is greatly encouraged and further serves to provide division between people. If you live in an area with little exposure to different demographics and all you see on the news are negative things, unsurprisingly, the view you have of that group of people will be negative.

Violent, aggressive and shallow/materialistic

Love & Hip Hop, *Real Housewives*, *Black Ink Crew New York* are all African American pseudo-'reality' shows that perpetuate aggression and materialism. There is a separate conversation to be had about the entertainment value of these shows, but what is clear is that African Americans are often painted in an unflattering light. Members of the cast are seemingly encouraged to fight with one another for entertainment. There is clearly an incentive for conflict and extreme drama. This is partly the formula of this breed of reality TV, but the hyper-characterised African American stereotype it perpetuates is destructive. This type of show and other negative narratives are particularly dangerous for a couple of reasons: they glamourise negative components of the culture (to be clear not every second of every episode is violent, just the most heightened scenes), and they support an idea of 'other' that leads to the conscious and subconscious justification of acts of brutality against the community. The idea that all Black people are loud, aggressive, and violent, and so are, therefore, likely to commit crimes or resist arrest, are key pillars of the detrimental narrative used to support the structural oppression that are in place against people of colour.

The danger in these narratives is not just that they are pejorative, but rather they again feed into a broader dehumanising ideology that Black people are inferior and less than others, conversely affirming notions of White supremacy. This prevailing narrative helps to justify the oppression of people of colour in all its forms, and therein lies its true malice.

In summary, we have the men, women, and children of the community labelled as violent, criminal, dangerous, aggressive, and superficial. But how are these narratives communicated? What are the vehicles for this viral spread?

Music and the Modern Minstrel Show

Music is a powerful and emotive tool. For thousands of years, humans all over the world have enjoyed and been inspired by music. It taps into our feelings in a very unique way and is a great form of expression. Music is a great way to communicate stories and messages, whether they be positive or negative. On the positive side, you have songs like Marvin Gaye's *What's Going On?* That comment on social injustices and global problems to Michael Jackson's *Earth Song,* which highlighted the huge environmental challenges facing the planet (that are still not being adequately addressed almost 20 years later). Of course, we have love songs, arguably the most universal of human pursuits, whether it's about falling in love or heartbreak, we all love a good love song.

However, we also know that music can have a less positive message. It is a key tool in shaping the minds of future generations to follow negative stereotypes. This revelation was seized upon in the early '90s with gangsta rap, a genre that began as protest music and a reflection of living in a dangerous and bleak environment that transformed into a multi-billion-dollar cash cow that also fed the beast of the negative stereotype. We have to look at why the initial pioneers that included the likes of Public Enemy and KRS-One who championed the struggle for progress disappeared only to be replaced by less progressive artists such as Lil Pump who focus on materialistic, misogynistic, and violent messages. This is not to minimise everyone's own prerogative for artistic expression but rather highlight that music with a specific narrative was promoted over a more positive type. The initial shift was subtle, but once the commercial and psychological impact was identified, hip-hop was pushed to the front of society.

Looking at the changing trend of popular music produced by the Diaspora from the late '80s to the present day, particularly from around the mid-'90s when hip-hop and R'n'B were deemed to be commercially optimal and prime for exploitation, you can see a clear shift in the type or sub-genre that is promoted—a very prominent sway from conscious rap to gangster rap. Almost in tandem, we saw a switch from largely more innocent love-based R'n'B to a more sexually charged variant. This is not to say that all prior forms of the genres were lost, but the emphasis and marketing budgets had clearly changed focus.

For me, the change in dynamics was particularly visible because I remember a time when hip-hop music was hard to find in record shops. Yes, back when there were physical record shops like Our Price or Tower Records, there were tiny sections filled with imports from the US, which you had to pay a premium for because of the shipping. Similarly, there was not much representation on the two music channels that were available in the late '90s, unsurprisingly, nor was there much activity in the mainstream charts. The popular weekly music show *Top of the Pops* aired every Friday, and once in a while, you would see songs like Mark Morrison's *Return of the Mack* or a song by Will Smith riding high in the charts, but it was not the norm.

Fast forward 10 years into the 2000s, and we see a breakthrough into the popular mainstream with a very bright and attractive brand of hip-hop, full of alluring violence, shining precious stones and metals, and attractive scantily clad women—this was a veritable attack on the senses. I imagine a lot of research went into the psychology of capturing people's attention with alluring imagery. Now, this in itself is not inherently bad. Bear with me. What I mean to say is people are allowed to have fun; they are allowed to like material things and enjoy sex. It could be argued that these things are part and parcel of being a Western person in the twenty-first century under the hand of capitalism. The issue, however, comes with the negative connotation of the narrative and imagery. The promotion and glamourisation of violence can feed into the psyche of those who consume it, particularly those who identify with it and then look to emulate it, leading to increased criminality and the solitary pursuit of material gain.

There are a couple of things to unpick here, the first being the important interconnectedness of the negative narratives perpetuated through music and the media that feed into a system of increased criminal activity and gang violence, Black-on-Black crime, and in turn, serves the prison-industrial complex.

The second is the depiction of success and means of achievement. The glamourisation of wealth as the pinnacle of success is prevalent across Western society and is a core pillar of the capitalist system. People need to consume to keep things rolling; material items are demonstrations of your wealth. Often, flagrant demonstrations of who has the most jewellery, the latest car, or the biggest house just feels like a contest of fragile egos. Those who can consume the most or demonstrate the potential to consume e.g. by showing off their wealth through cars, houses, and holidays are doing better in life. One of the issues with this approach is it does not provide much guidance on how to get this wealth nor does it leave much room for less material and arguably more important measures of success like being happy, feeling fulfilled and sharing experiences with loved ones.

Following the 'get rich by any means necessary' approach (or *Get Rich or Die Tryin'*—50 Cent) can lead to negative routes to wealth e.g. crime. If becoming a drug dealer is the only route to self-determination and perceived societal success, that can't be a good thing. We cannot have the younger generations risking their life or the lives of others to obtain material wealth, all while continuing to perpetuate a negative cycle.

The evolution of urban music, particularly hip-hop is a cause for concern. From its inception as a form of protest, we have seen it mutate into different and seemingly more aggressive versions, looking at original protest and conscious hip-hop to gangsta rap of the '90s and beyond to what we see nowadays with 'Drill' music. Of course, there are other versions that are not always as violent or aggressive, but those mentioned are the most popular. The direction of travel is clear; if the path is followed, I'm not sure I want to know what comes next.

The multiple prongs of the urban music machine are as strategically nuanced as that of the mass incarceration system are. While on the one hand advocating and encouraging violence, crime, and materialistic wealth, it has also proved to be a huge money spinner for music labels, increasing wealth for label owners and executives who are rarely Black, while destabilising Black communities.

Appropriation Without Representation

Appropriation or appreciation? This is an ongoing debate that is usually ultimately determined by your subjective view on the given case in hand. However, there have been many examples that are perhaps more objectively clear, particularly from bygone eras in the music world, particularly in peri-Motown era, when the likes of Big Mama Thornton's *Hound Dog, Baby,* Arthur Neal Gunter's *Let's Play House*, and Lloyd Price's *Lawdy Miss Clawdy* had their music stolen (covered) by White artists like Elvis.[210] This is, of course, much less common in the present day.

Appropriation in the world of visual art can be less clear as inspiration is a big part of the artistic process; it's harder to be objective about appropriation. There are examples of patterns that have been used by European desires that have been suggested as appropriation, but where is that line for general inspiration? A cue that is often missed is acknowledgement, a formal recognition of the source of inspiration; this can go a long way to easing tensions. However, the main problem with the appropriation dynamic in general is the power-play that is at hand i.e. the notion that White supremacy dictates—that it is able to pick and choose what it wants to take without consequence, as we saw with past examples in music.

Racism and Bias in the Media

The majority of people get their information from the media. Before the internet took over, newspapers and news channels were the best bet to find out what you needed to know about what was going on in the world. With such a significant sphere of influence, this industry is extremely powerful. Many people knowingly or unknowingly hold what they consume via the media as gospel. As such a level of assumed credibility comes along with it, we trust the news, in many cases, implicitly. This can be problematic when a source considered to be objective, credible and fact-based is consistently telling us that one group of people are negative and dangerous. This is another way to dehumanise certain demographics and condition the wider majority to tacitly accept race-based oppression.

The press in the UK and US have become more subtle in recent times with regards to what could be perceived to be racist content, but it is still present if you read between the lines. The more conservative outlets like the *Daily Mail*, *Express* or *Sun* in the UK regularly have politically charged and Islamophobic content, driving the narrative of 'the other' and peddling fears of immigrants stealing jobs and overloading the fragile public sector. Newspaper coverage also shows flares of racism with the way stories about Black people are positioned, regularly with a negative slant.

The Dylan Roof massacre is a prime example of the selective sleight of hand the Western media tends to employ with regards to acts of White domestic terrorism. On 17 June 2015, 21-year-old Roof massacred nine African Americans inside a church in South Carolina. Media coverage reported Roof as mentally ill, a 'loner', a 'kid', and 'one hateful person'.[211] The theme here is of one community minimising negative instances to the individual or individualism vs. anything negative individual acts in the Black community being ascribed collectively to the entire community. Thus, when a White person commits a horrifying act, it is a one-off, an outlier with no broader context or agenda, coupled with an attempt to rationalise and humanise the individual with soft descriptive language. This is in stark contrast to how African Americans who have been murdered by the police are described. 12-year-old Tamir Rice was described as a '20-year-old' by police officers; Trayvon Martin was 'as much responsible' as George Zimmerman because he was wearing a hoody; Eric Garner sold loose cigarettes.[212,213] The extent to which the media will vilify African American victims and protect White murderers is at times outstanding.

An example given by Chelsea and England star Raheem Sterling about his former teammates Tosin Adarabioyo, who is Black, and Phil Foden, a White player, clearly demonstrates the racially driven agenda of some media outlets. The *Daily Mail*, the country's second-largest tabloid newspaper, reported on the two players buying homes for their respective mothers: Adarabioyo was chastised for spending £2.5 million pounds on a house 'despite having never started a Premier League match', while Foden was praised as a 'starlet' for spending £2 million on a 'home for his mum'. It doesn't take much investigating to spot the difference.[214,215]

Following the police shooting of unarmed Mark Duggan in August 2011, which sparked nationwide riots across the UK, the image used by the media of Mark was carefully cropped. The picture used shows a stern-faced man in a hooded jacket, someone that the public could easily vilify. However, the full picture is Mark holding a heart that pays respect to his dead daughter who was stillborn—no wonder he wasn't smiling. Clearly, a picture of a grieving father is much harder to hate than a potential criminal, something the media knew very well.

Reflecting on these examples in the UK, reporting on people of colour shows a clear pattern. There are numerous examples of media outlets unfairly portraying negative and often racist narratives. We saw the harassment and targeting faced by Megan Markle, a soon-to-be and then actual member of the royal family, for no other significant reason than her being mixed race.

A report into US media coverage of poverty by race shows how inaccurate negative narratives are perpetuated. The study showed that African American families made up 59% of those portrayed as poor on the news while actually making up 27% of lower-income American families; conversely, White families made up only 17% of poor families covered on the news, compared to the 66% of lower-income families they actually make up.[216]

A Media Matters study found that late-night crime reporting between 18 August and 13 December 2014, on news stations (WCBS, WNBC, WABC, and WNYW) disproportionately covered African Americans in crimes of murder, theft, and assault. The stations covered African American suspects in 74% of murder reports, 84% of theft stories and 73% of assaults. This is in contrast to New York City Police Department statistics that show African Americans were only suspects for 54% of murders, 55% of thefts, and 49% of assaults.[217] This is a very real example of how a powerful tool is being used to unfairly and negatively shape the narrative of people in the Diaspora. The same media scare tactics that were used to kick-start the war on drugs are still being employed decades later to dehumanise African Americans.

The problems with racist media were put on show once again in the coverage of the 2022 Russian invasion of Ukraine. The BBC showed a comment from a Ukrainian official stating, 'It's very emotional for me because I see European people with blue eyes and blonde hair being killed.' Meanwhile, a CBS news reporter noted, 'This is a relatively civilised, relatively European—I have to choose those words carefully too—the city where you wouldn't expect that or hope it is going to happen.' An NBC correspondent said, 'These are Christians; they're White; they're very similar people.'[218] These are all liberal Western media outlets with the same clear message: Ukrainians are similar enough to us in the West to warrant significant outrage, not like those from Brown and Black countries.

Lack of Representation

Sterling K. Brown became the first African American to win best actor at the Golden Globe Awards, for his performance in the hit TV show *This is Us*, a historic moment in the world of television. In his acceptance speech, Sterling thanked the casting director Dan Fogelman for writing a role created specifically for a 'Black man', as opposed to just giving a brother a break, casting him in a role that was not tailor-made.[219]

This sparked thoughts of past conversations I've had about the importance of diverse representation and, critically, the importance of positive diverse representation, in this instance, in the mainstream media. In my opinion, it's key to have a fair reflection of the demographic breakdown of your society on your mainstream media channels, allowing people to see themselves on screen and in print in a positive light. Why? Because it shows people who may feel and actually be marginalised that they are valued by said society. Fair and positive representation says that you are important; you too are an integral part of our cultural tapestry.

Perhaps even more significant is the constructive impact positive characters and role models can have on young people growing up, especially if those role models aren't readily available in real life. You can imagine the positive effect a female doctor of colour on a hit soap would have on a young girl from the same background—consciously or subconsciously the seed will be sown that 'I can be that person.' I am not suggesting that we solely rely on mainstream media for role models; entertainers are often terrible role models; however, these avenues have broad access to many people and could inspire them.

The flip side of this point is having negative representation and the messages that can send. Sadly, the majority of what is communicated about people of colour in the mainstream media is negative, either negative news stories involving crime or film and TV roles focused on gang life, e.g. *Top Boy* (although a well-made and entertaining show). Looking at the urban music scene, we again see from a mainstream perspective, a skewed focus on negative stereotypes of gang culture and video girls.

The implications of this can be severe. If this is all young people from minority backgrounds are exposed to, it can drive negative aspirations. Glamourising gang culture can drive misguided hopes of emulating a dangerous lifestyle for those who are easily influenced or may just want a way to try to transcend a difficult environment.

Moreover, the impact on the perceptions of wider society should be considered. Even in a relatively integrated country like England, the separation of the traditional English person and those from ethnic minorities is quite stark. You only have to visit the Home Counties, Shires, or any town and assess the level of diversity and integration. The problem here is that the only exposure that a lot of these people get to those from different backgrounds is through the media, so when that prism is overwhelmingly negative, you can see how damaging stereotypes are formed, which can lead to difficulties in fostering an integrated society. A prime example (though it was not the sole cause) of this was the voting pattern in Brexit; the clear contrast between those from mixed urban communities who had real experience of minorities, compared with those from less diverse areas who manifested their experience vicariously through the media was telling. I can attest to the power of these negative stereotypes having seen how people behave if I'm wearing a hoody...

In the case of Sterling K. Brown, not only do we have positive representation, but we also have positive representation that has been professionally recognised. This is an added layer of significance because separate to the stellar performance of Brown, we are seeing a positive minority image being rewarded. This sends the subtle message that we as a society are starting to value positive images of people of colour, in contrast to the typically negative images portrayed, for example, Denzel Washington's Oscar-winning performance as a bad cop in *Training Day*.

Despite the need for broader representation, there can be resistance to it from White audiences. The reaction in England to more diverse Christmas adverts from major supermarket chain Sainsbury's in 2020 was a prime example. Certain White people took to Twitter en masse to express their disappointment that a Black family was chosen for these adverts because, of course, they could only be enjoyed if the fictional families looked like them. This was a wholesome, peaceful, Black version of a 2.4 children family, no trauma in sight, but it did not strike the right chord with some of White Britain. A similar sentiment of resentment and upset was shown by the British public when *Britain's Got Talent* showcased a piece of performance art by dance troupe Diversity created to honour George Floyd.

Representation is important and the sphere of entertainment (sports, music, film etc.) is where people of colour have had the biggest opportunity to shine, but we need to expand this to other industries. I hope Sterling's success breeds more of the same. This achievement is proof that people want to see more diverse positive representation—and it just might win you an award!

Beauty Is in the Eye of the Controller (Editor)

It could be argued that the beauty narrative is a superficial one. Surely what is of most importance is someone's character, personality, who they are as a person. This is true, but what is also true is that we live in a society where beauty is highly venerated, particularly for women. The idea of beauty is a narrative and, as with other narratives, is communicated through different forms of media. Beauty is in the eye of the beholder…or as I see it, is in who controls what the eye can see; by that I mean who has the power to determine what you can see, who controls the media, the channels for communication of the beauty narrative…the perceived standards of beauty.

I remember being at a family friend's engagement party. She was a Black British girl marrying a Black British guy and the majority of guests were Black or mixed race with a sprinkling of White faces. One of the White faces was my then-girlfriend who in my eyes is a beautiful woman. This sentiment was shared by a young Black boy who could not have been any older than four. He was totally obsessed, besotted, head over heels. I was pretty sure I could hold my own against this mini-Casanova, despite his cuteness, but it did make me wonder, why was he so enamoured with her? Was it because she was different... perhaps enigmatic, irresistibly engaging (she would say so), or was it because even at such a tender age, he'd already been programmed, like so many others, to think that the face of beauty was fair?

Growing up in the West, it took me a while to question and interrogate what I and the society around me considered to be generally 'beautiful'. Because of the subjective nature of this subject, I feel I need to keep 'beauty/beautiful' in inverted commas. I think it's clear to most people that the ideal of 'beauty' in the West is promoted to be a particular type of woman with typical features, for example, straight hair, thin nose. A mainstream American news show discussing the ideal of 'beauty', highlighted actress Erica Durance (Lois Lane from the Superman show *Smallville*) as a good example of true 'beauty'—but if that is the ideal of Western beauty, where does that leave those who do not fit the mould? Where does that leave people of the Diaspora?

For me, this narrative makes sense as an important tool of the current Western patriarchal power structure that promotes a particular ideal of 'beauty' to help maintain the status quo. But is it *true*? Without going into any empirical data, a quick look across mainstream media gives a pretty clear indication of what Western society considers to be 'beautiful'. Flip through some fashion magazines, take a look at the models, the so-called pinnacle of 'beauty'; watch TV, go to the movies, check the leading ladies or so-called eye candy, and the theme is pretty clear. Some may argue that this is just proportional representation. We live in a predominantly

White society; of course, the majority of images are going to be White.

However, it does seem that the representation of women of colour in the mainstream media and platforms of traditional beauty are few and far between. This for me was aptly reflected in the fact that the great Naomi Campbell had to campaign for more diversity on the runway scene. I think this is further reflected across the West. If you were to ask the average man on the street to name five beautiful women of colour, the likely response would be US-focused and probably include Beyoncé. Challenge people to think of people in the UK and I think most people would falter. Perhaps it's not an issue of colour at all, but rather something more universal, geometry. I've read opinions and pseudo-scientific analysis that would suggest that objective 'beauty' is more to do with symmetry, distance, and proportion, rather than the shade of one's skin. A closer look at these supposedly objective investigations, unsurprisingly translates into code for a thinner nose, smaller lips and straight hair, which subsequently brings you quite quickly back to race. This idea is reflected in the women of colour who are considered to be 'beautiful'; the Naomi Campbells, Beyoncé Knowles-Carters, Thandiwe Newtons, etc. all have what could be considered to be Caucasian leaning features, with 70s supermodel Iman being described as a 'White woman dipped in Chocolate'.

Of course, the link between colour and perceived beauty is historic, as part of the oppressive controls placed on Black and Brown people throughout the ages. Perpetuating the myth that Black was bad and White more 'beautiful', nobler, and godlier, was an important method of control. Looking back at the transatlantic slave trade and the positions of privilege gifted to the fairer enslaved people or 'house negroes' was an example of how being fairer or closer to White was better. This has continued through to the present day with lighter-skinned Black girls (and to an extent guys) deemed automatically to be more attractive by most (not all)! One of my favourite films is *Coming to America*, and it always amazed me that a dark-skinned African prince came to America to find the love of his life, only to fall for the fair, long-haired Lisa, over her darker-skinned sister Patrice. Again, it's easy to reel off the names of fairer women of colour who have claimed the title of 'beauty' over the years, from Lisa Bonet and Halle Berry to the more contemporary Zendaya. This is a continuation of the same story: if you want to be considered beautiful, you need to be fair with more Western features.

Brown paper bag test...

As much as it pains me to discuss, the notion of fairer skin and beauty is also clearly highlighted with the concept of 'colourism' (the idea of racism within a race, based on those with fairer skin being seen as superior to those who are darker) and the phenomena of skin-bleaching that is one of the sad consequences of this mentality—something that is present in communities of colour all over the world. It breaks my heart to see people with patchy uneven skin tones that are clearly the result of a lightening procedure. This narrative can also be seen in Asian communities. When walking through Bangkok airport in Thailand, I was shocked to see the amount of skin-lightening products advertised. Chinese people often protect themselves from the sun for fear of tanning. The association, as I understand it, is that darker skin is associated with working in the fields and so a lower social class, compared with lighter skin, which can be protected from the sun indoors. Post-colonial hangovers of this 'beauty' standard can also be seen in India, other parts of Asia, Central and South America, Africa, and the Caribbean.

So far, I've focused on women; that is probably some inherent reflection of my own partially conditioned misogynistic mindset, driven by a patriarchal society that says that beauty and women are intrinsically linked. It's hard for me to shake this association even though I consider myself to be a 'feminist'. I feel I can speak more freely on the male perspective as a Black man. I believe the focus on 'beautiful'/handsome men in the West is driven toward White men, with the obvious exceptions e.g. Will Smith or Idris Elba. Two important points for me regarding the gender difference are that as a man, society has deemed it less important for me to be attractive in order to be valued or successful, and the shade of my skin also seems to be less important. I see more guys with darker complexions in mainstream media than I do my mahogany sisters. This is undoubtedly linked to male privilege.

What Does It All Mean? Impact of Negative Narratives and Beauty Standards

Is perceived 'beauty' of any real importance? The adage goes 'beauty is only skin deep'; moreover, we are taught that true beauty lies within. While I believe this to be the case, I do think there are some very real implications for those not deemed to meet Western society's ideal of 'beauty'.

Self-esteem

The main area of importance for me is self-esteem. If you fail to see an appropriate representation of yourself or people that you can relate to you via the usual channels of beauty, e.g. films or magazines, you may begin to question your own beauty and subsequently your self-worth. I think this is particularly pertinent for women as we live in a patriarchal world, where for hundreds if not thousands of years, the value of a woman has been intrinsically linked to their perceived beauty or sex appeal. So, if you have been told that a large amount of your worth is derived from how attractive you are, and you then feel that you are not attractive, you can see how this could have a significant impact on your self-esteem. If this is the case, and depending on the severity of the impact, this could clearly have wider effects in other aspects of life.

Another, more practical implication of not being perceived to be 'beautiful' is finding a partner and potentially love. Attempting to view this from a perspective of a woman of colour, if you are not deemed to be quite aligned with the societal consensus of 'beauty', then you may find it harder to meet someone. We are all exposed to the same conditioning and messaging, consciously and subconsciously as such men are also being told that the ideal of 'beauty' is a Caucasian. I know there is an issue in the UK, at least, with the perception that some (by no means all) Black men would rather date outside the race. The data on marriage in the UK, however, does not support this, with Black men and women much more likely to marry one another than people outside of the race.

In addition, the majority of White men would be less likely to date a woman of colour than someone of their own ethnic background, perhaps unsurprising, people tend to date and marry within their race. I watched a great documentary, *Is Love Racist?* by Emma Dabiri that highlighted these themes. As part of the show, around 5,000 people were surveyed on the physical features of their preferred partners. According to the survey, 35% of White people said they would never date a Black person, whereas 10% of Black people wouldn't date a White person.[220] The rough outcome of this social equation is that there would be fewer options for women of colour who are trying to meet someone outside of their race.

Perception of being less than

Another consideration is the subtle message being sent that if your beauty is less than that of White Westerners, you are also less than. This is a subtle but, I believe, an important additional consequence of the White supremacy narrative. Wrapped within this, we have other related items such as 'nude' make-up being pink in tone; this has been the status quo up until recently. The message is: 'Your value is not worth recognising and the only true 'nude' skin tone looks like ours. We are the most important.'

There is also an argument around how being seen as unattractive contributes to a narrative of dehumanisation that helps to justify the discriminatory actions and systems in place within society. If narratives communicate that people of colour are less important and less worthy, it makes it easier to ignore humanitarian issues like police brutality. The beauty narrative helps perpetuate this, particularly with women, in a patriarchal society where a woman's value is often intrinsically connected to her perceived beauty. If people of colour are less beautiful; then, by proxy, they are of less value and so command less societal sympathy and attention.Maybe things aren't so bad. Popular culture, musically at least, is heavily driven by the 'urban' world, which regularly highlights certain beautiful women of colour. The Beyoncés, Rihannas and Nikis are considered global 'beauties', and we're starting to see some progress for those of darker complexion with the rise of Lupita Nyong'o and Jourdan Dunn. While I believe we are making progress, I think the current status quo is clear: White beauty is purported as best, followed by those who are fairer and have Western features. We are a long way off a level playing field where the average woman of colour is considered objectively beautiful by the masses, in the West and beyond.

The idea of being less than can be communicated through the 'positive' as well as absence or 'negative'. While communicating that the Western beauty standard is the ideal and so anyone who doesn't measure up, or is without is not beautiful is negative; we also see hypersexualisation of Black women as a 'positive' way to communicate a message of being 'less than'. Both approaches affirm Western beauty standards as the ideal.

So, what's the issue? Can't Black women be perceived as sexy? Of course, they can, but the problem is when they are only seen that way, one-dimensional, without any other redeeming attributes. The idea that Black women are somewhat inherently promiscuous man-eaters can be seen in how some Black female singers are positioned in the industry. The overt sex appeal connected to the likes of Nicki Minaj, Megan Thee Stallion and Rihanna, compared to Taylor Swift is stark. The concept of sex selling is nothing new and by no means reserved for Black females but is disproportionately implemented in this demographic.

Interestingly, under the purview of White supremacy, Black women are subjected to a dual-pronged approach: being told they, on the one hand, do not meet the beauty standard while, on the other hand, being hypersexualised. We know from the level of rape during slavery that physical desire was never an issue, although power dynamics were also at play. This seemingly contraindicatory dichotomy of being both unattractive, yet lusted over, still serves to dehumanise and devalue the Black woman. If women are objectified for sex, it becomes easier to overlook and ignore their needs, and mistreat them. A similar thing can be said for the narrative of Black women being loud or aggressive. Something that is a surprising assertion to make against arguably the most marginalised and left behind group in society—there may be a distinct survival need linked to being forthright.

Black men also fall victim to dehumanisation through hypersexuality. The focus and attention on the Black male penis have driven psychological insecurity among some White men for centuries but has also been used to restrict i.e. the Black man is no more than a well-endowed sex-crazed individual. Reducing the Black man to his sexual appendage or physicality is another method of dehumanisation that has been used to justify discrimination.

Self-destruction

The cycle is insidious in its self-destructive nature. Convincing people to buy into a system of their own destruction is somewhat inspired. The collateral fallout of the negative image is self-hate, to such a degree that we also buy into the narrative of being sub-human—low enough to kill without remorse or much consideration. The ease with which we can bring harm to one another from the same background but are reticent to do so with someone from a different background speaks volumes. Following decades of police brutality, you would think there would be more ill will towards that common or consistent enemy than to one another, but it is not the case. There are relatively few mentions of fighting the police but numerous ones of killing a 'nigga' or an 'op'. This is connected to those who control the negative image and stereotype and encourage the cycle of self-hate: it's okay to kill each other but keep it within your community.

Tied to the self-hate narrative of the Black male is the degradation of the Black female. The popularised view of the 'bitch' or 'video ho' is a modern-day take on an age-old narrative of the over-sexualised Black female. This story that was once used to blame Black women for the rape and abuse they suffered at the hands of their slave masters continues today.

Making Things Better

Narrative control

A critical step is taking control of our narrative, ensuring that the media representation of the community is not the current unbalanced negative version. This means showing all the great components of our make-up, from the range of different professions we contribute to and roles we play e.g. doctor, accountant, artist, mentor, youth worker, father, brother, friend, daughter, inventor, lawyer and business owner, as well as the entertainment and sports roles that are well-known. It will seem obvious to some, but perhaps not to all, but we are way more than rappers, athletes, and criminals. We cannot rely on others to perpetuate positive narratives for us, but we can communicate positive narratives for ourselves.

How do we execute narrative control? Well, part of the journey is having our own channels on platforms so we can have the final say. I've seen lots of great positive Instagram and other social media pages that communicate the positive and diverse breadth of our community. We need to leverage the opportunities that technology is creating to tell our own stories. You can literally create your own YouTube channel and post content, or build a website for free. In addition, modern platforms like Netflix are open to different content than traditional broadcasters because their model is to appeal to as many people as possible. With their self-directed method of viewing, they don't need to worry about 'upsetting' certain groups or being challenged if the content is not meeting the needs of the majority. The days of using TV schedules (linear broadcasting) with shows to please the general population are gone. We know that this is the future: people want to view whatever they are interested in when they want to watch (on demand).

This self-directed control should not stop with video content but should also be reflected in the written word with magazines and books. Why wait for a *GQ* special on Black men? Let's have our own magazine dedicated to it.

Broader and more positive representation in mainstream outlets

In the outlets we don't control, we also need more diverse and positive stories told. There is a space for the *Top Boy* type of story because that is a genuine reality for people, but it is not the only reality. Even with that type of drug-based gang story, there is so much scope to approach it from more nuanced angles. How about we take a look at some of the underlying social causes of ghettoisation and lack of opportunity that feed into a climate of criminality? Or take a look at the broader drug trade and how these drugs manage to find their way into these neighbourhoods? Or how the policing is vastly different for this type of crime depending on your ethnic background and the area you live in?

We do need to challenge the mainstream broadcasters (Sky, HBO, BBC, ITV, Channel 4, Netflix, Amazon) to do more, and there have been some positive signs of that with shows like *Insecure* with Issa Rae, a multi-dimensional Black woman who is figuring life out but is not bowing to the usual tropes of violence, hypersexuality, ratchetness, or anything else negative.

We also have *Black-ish,* from Kenya Barris and starring Anthony Anderson the father of the family, a successful advertising executive and his wife Bow (Rainbow) played by Tracee Ellis Ross who is a successful surgeon, portrays the life of a more modern and affluent African American family, akin to a modern-day *Cosby Show*. The family tackle contemporary issues of race, while also reflecting on historical challenges that being Black in America brings, even with some financial status there to protect you. Again, this is the Black family doing well in a positive light.

Special mention to *I May Destroy You* from Michaela Coel, which is a gripping portrayal of sexuality, sexual abuse and mental health told through the eyes of a young Black woman in London. These are real stories, consisting of three-dimensional characters, who have thoughts, feelings, and conflicts. Not just base-level, tired storytelling about the guy with guns from the end.

As discussed in the Economics chapter, it is important to stretch beyond representation alone. Representation has its merit and is key to narrative shaping, but we need to be mindful of being left with somewhat superficial gestures of increased TV representation in supermarket ads while deeper more meaningful change has not taken place. Broader representation across our screens won't mean much without the tangible systemic societal change underneath. There is little point in having Mo Gilligan host the Brit Awards if our youth continue to be excluded from school at a disproportional rate.

A balanced diet

Ensure we are careful about what we consume and ensure that it is balanced. The visual and written content we consume, just like the food we eat, needs to be healthy and balanced. That means there can be room for the occasional treat, which from a content perspective, I would describe as materialistic hip-hop about money, jewellery and violence or a series of *Power*, but this should not be the staple. The problem is if this type of superficial content forms too big a portion of your visual and verbal intake, it will have an impact on your mentality, and the impact will not be positive. Just like if you based your diet solely around fast food, you would become overweight and unhealthy. We need to take time to consciously monitor what we are consuming and ensure we are basing it on nourishing content which is positive and healthy. Are you reading about positive things? Are you learning new skills? Are you listening to music that will uplift you and make you feel good, promote a sense of community and love? These are the types of things that should form the majority of what we consume.

A greater understanding of self

It is much harder to tell a dog it is a cat when it knows it is a dog. An area of general importance for the Black community, not just linked to narrative control, is having a deep understanding of who you are and where you've come from. A greater sense of self makes it much easier to challenge false and negative stereotypes. If I understand the great things my ancestors have contributed to the world from ancient civilisations like Kush all the way through to modern technology advances like the PC monitor and Super Soaker (brought smiles to the faces of many children), I know my value and I know it is more than the dangerous criminal that certain societal narratives portray.

We should all know our history to understand where we come from, that k it's more than slavery and civil rights movements. It's imperative that we understand the contributions that have been made by those before us, so we feel inspired to continue to make significant contributions to the world moving forward, to know that we should stand tall and be proud of who we are and vigorously challenge those who would seek to belittle us.

The Interconnectedness of Media and Entertainment

We see clear connections between the world of entertainment with regards to lack of narrative control and ownership, as we do in the broader economic setting. It is very hard to set your own narrative when you lack ownership and are not in control of it. Equally, the best way to improve representation is by having greater control of the spaces you want to be represented in. We see in more detail how the perpetuation of negative and violent narratives feeds into and fuels the dehumanisation that is required for police brutality, exclusion and oppressive systems like mass incarceration. We also see how Western beauty standards can fuel an internalised sense of inferiority, while also reinforcing a dehumanised view of Black people. These themes will also come up in the final chapters as we delve into the sporting world and take a look at the psychological and mental health impact of those in the Diaspora.

Chapter 8: Sports, Sports and the Plantation

'But as I write these words now, I cannot stand and sing the National Anthem. I have learned that I remain a Black in a White world.'[221]
– Jackie Robinson

In this chapter:

Challenges

- Discrimination on and off the field
- Lack of representation off the field in positions of influence

Making things better

- Increased representation off the field
- Policy change and greater protection

I love sports, pretty much all sports, but my first true love was football. I don't remember exactly what age I was when

I started to kick a ball, but definitely not long after I started walking. It wasn't too long after that I started my journey to become a lifelong Arsenal fan, receiving my first-ever kit on my seventh birthday.

I was fortunate enough to have a long and happy 'career' playing at different levels through school and university and beyond. In addition to football, I was the 200-metre borough champion in secondary school and played tennis and basketball. One of the things I love most about sports is that it is a great leveller. No matter where you come from, your ethnic background or financial status, the field, court, or pitch was a place where your talent, effort, and passion are the only things that matter. With football in particular, the great global game, you literally only need a ball to play—jumpers for goalposts were definitely the norm for me growing up. Its accessibility is a big part of its global appeal; it transcends any prohibitively expensive equipment or facilities. From Brazilian favelas to the Australian outback, anybody can get involved. Sports for the Black community has always been one of the main routes to prosperity, financial freedom and escape from 'the ends'.

There are two broad areas of improvement in the sporting world: athletes who are still subjected to racial abuse on and off the field and the lack of representation off the field, from managers and coaches all the way through the organisational structure to the ownership level.

Racism in Sport

In the current era, we are fortunate enough to see people of colour in many different arenas demonstrating excellence, winning trophies and entertaining fans the world over. However, it is important to acknowledge that this was not always the case; racial barriers have historically been in place, preventing Black people from participating in professional sports in the first place. It wasn't always a given, or even an option in years gone by.

Despite the fact that people of colour are regularly the stars of the team and in some sports like basketball in the US make up the vast majority of the entire league, athletes and players are still victims of racial abuse while playing and online after the games. So confused is the logic of these racist 'fans' that you can find people abusing their own players despite the fact these players may be the very reason the team is successful. During the 2020 European Championship (played in 2021), we saw English fans boo the national team for taking the knee in solidarity against racism, only to be cheering minutes later when a Black player scored.

Sadly, this is still very much a contemporary reality. In October 2019, the England national team was playing an international qualifier against Bulgaria in Sofia. Part of the Bulgarian stadium was already closed as a punishment for previous racist acts by Bulgarian fans, so with the number of Black players in the England team, an incident was anticipated. UEFA, the European football governing body, had set up guidelines to manage any racially abusive actions e.g. chants from fans to players. If a sufficient amount of racial abuse is detected in a game, the referee would stop the game and a stadium-wide announcement would be issued to warn the fans. Three stoppages and the game would be abandoned. The game was stopped twice due to racial slurs coming from the fans, including monkey chants and Nazi salutes. The captain of the Bulgarian team pleaded with the fans to stop the chants, knowing one more stoppage would end the game. A lot of the more vocal fans left halfway through, allowing the game to continue. This was another example of a bittersweet approach to legislative challenge to racial reform.[222] The 3-step framework from UEFA is, on one hand, an example of a formal process to tackle racism in football. In previous decades, players would just have to endure it or choose to self-sacrifice and leave the game themselves. However, when we look at the specific punishment doled out to the Bulgarian national team for the incident, we see it is only a paltry £65,000. That effectively is the significance UEFA places on almost abandoning an international football match because of racial abuse; this low valuation is at the root of the problem. If it is of minuscule importance to the governing bodies charged with running the game, then how can we expect fans to take it seriously?

This type of event is not limited to countries with low Black populations; fans of the English national team are not necessarily any better. The summer of 2021 brought Europe's best national teams to England for the European Championships. Against the backdrop of the COVID-19 pandemic and lockdowns, a promising young English team were one of the favourites to win the tournament, not only because of their talented squad, containing star Black players such as Raheem Sterling, Marcus Rashford, Bukayo Saka, and Jadon Sancho but also because key games would be played at Wembley—including the semi-final and final—providing a massive home field advantage. This tournament was unique for many reasons, not just because of the location and genuine chance of England winning the trophy for the first time in its history but also for the undercurrent of activism and ultimately the nation's true colours being shown.[223]

Following on from the Black Lives Matter-inspired protests of the previous year, Premier League teams along with the England team had been taking the knee before kick-off in protest against racism and all forms of discrimination. This continued during the tournament to the dismay of some England fans who booed their own players taking the knee—the very same fans who cheered when Black players scored, most notably Sterling who scored several key goals aiding England's route to the final. The abuse directed at their own players was a clear precursor of what was to come.

After reaching the final, a historic feat in itself for England, the tournament would end on a sour note. After taking the lead against Italy, England were *pegged back,* and the game went to penalties. For anyone who is unfamiliar, penalties are a cruel way to end the game because there will be at least one villain, the player who misses the penalty and loses the game for his team, or in some cases, multiple villains. The shot from 12 yards can seem straightforward enough, but there is a significant element of luck, even for the most seasoned player. If the goalkeeper happens to guess right, even the best penalties can be saved. Moreover, the psychological pressure of the real game environment is something that cannot be replicated in a training session.

Villain is a harsh and unfair word for those who miss because you have to be brave enough to put yourself forward for the task and take on the responsibility and jeopardy of potentially missing. In this shoot-out, three young Black English Lions put themselves forward to try and take their country to victory—particularly brave when you consider how young these players were, none beyond their early 20s. So, in the cauldron of a packed Wembley stadium, with the weight of the nation on their backs, they stepped forward. As if written by a mischievous god of fate, all three Black English players missed, and England lost the tournament. The subsequent torrent of online racial abuse was to be expected by anyone Black in Britain and anyone who had the most simplistic understanding of the country's issues with race. It is worth reiterating that Black players were integral in getting the team to the final and they were the ones brave enough and deemed capable enough by the manager to take the penalties, but all of that counted for nothing—they were the villains of the show.

The examples of present-day racism in football are not limited to national team games. There are also examples in Europe's top club leagues. A Manchester City fan was banned from football for five years for shouting racist abuse at Raheem Sterling, a player for his own team! This is not an example from the 1970s; this happened in 2019![224] In a Premier League game between Manchester City and Chelsea in 2018, Raheem Sterling received racial abuse from fans, being called a 'Fucking Black cunt'.[225] This is still common in today's game. If we look abroad to the European leagues, we also see that the problem is persistent and widespread. Italy's top division Series A is regularly a venue for racial abuse towards players of colour. Between August 1, 2019, and March 1, 2020, there were 58 cases of racial discrimination that impacted Italian football and sport in general, according to *Cronache di ordinario razzismo*

(*Chronicles of Ordinary Racism*), a website that keeps track of institutional and everyday racism in Italy since 2011.[226]

While racism in games is abhorrent, there was a time when racism prevented people of colour from actually playing sports at all. Taking a look at American sports and the history of segregation, African Americans were banned from playing sports with White people, which lead to the creation of separate 'Negro Leagues'. Several leagues were set up, beginning with the National Negro League in 1920 and ending with integration in the 1950s.[227] These African American leagues met the demand for baseball among the African American community that segregation prevented.

Interestingly, from the US perspective of segregated leagues, integration was in some ways a poisoned chalice, destroying Black-owned teams and leagues. Separate leagues may not be essential for progress, but ownership and representation at different levels of sports organisations are. Ironically, this problem was overcome by segregated leagues.

Play Your Position

The discrimination suffered by players of colour can also come in more subtle forms and from internal members of staff. This is a more subtle observation but a valid one, nonetheless. In American Football, a sport dominated by African Americans, the most important position on the team is an area with particularly low African American representation: the quarterback (QB).

Historically, African Americans make up nearly 70% of all NFL players, but only around 17% of quarterbacks (QBs).[228] If you are familiar with the sport, you'll know that this is the person who dictates the entire game, someone whose contribution will typically dictate whether a team will win or lose a game. So, why then does this sport have such disparity, in such a crucial position of the team? After all, African Americans are good enough to play practically every other role. The quarterback is not only the most important player on the team, but he also plays the role that is considered to be the most intellectually challenging because he has to remember all of the 'plays' (different game strategies) for his team. This supposed high mental workload has been considered to be better suited to White players because, after all, when it comes to intelligence, you would not want to leave that to a Black player.

As mentioned, there are usually a small number of African American QBs. These players are often lauded more for their athleticism than they are for their intellectual game in keeping with the narrative. In fact, a study by a popular US sports magazine *Sports Illustrated* between 1998–2007 looked at the descriptions used for African American QBs compared to their White counterparts. The study showed this effect, with African Americans praised for their athleticism (e.g. an impressive specimen) and criticised for their lack of intellect, vice versa for the White players, lauded for being 'real students of the game'.[229,230]

The motive behind this micro-segregation is not only practical but also psychological and symbolic. American Football is often regarded as 'America's Game'; it is the nation's favourite sport. For a country built on White supremacy, it is a little hard to accept that America's game is best played by those who are supposedly inferior. The domination of White players in its key position is an effective way to balance things out. In addition, the QB is the lead role, leading the team of African Americans, so while there are fewer of 'us', we are still in charge. The psychology of this should not be underestimated.

Although less obvious, the assessment or notion that Black players should only play certain roles is also pervasive in the world of football (soccer). Black players are seen in and encouraged to play most positions, but the area of the pitch that arguably requires the most intelligence and creativity is where you are least likely to see a Black player, that is the number 10 role, just behind the striker. This position is deployed less often in recent times, but during its hey-day, it was rarely a position considered acceptable for Black players. This is funny because it is common for Black players to play the position just in front as a main striker. Here, the attributes of strength and pace, usually associated with Black players, are embraced. In my opinion, the reasons why Black players are guided away from the number 10 spot and to a lesser extent, deeper central midfield roles is based on the archaic and inaccurate notion that Black players do not have the creativity or intelligence to play those roles. In addition, these roles often garner the limelight and attention, so similarly, from a psychological perspective, if there are going to be a lot of Black players on the pitch, we will at least keep them away from certain pivotal positions.

This narrative, like many aspects of racism, is not just limited to the coaching staff and management but also perpetuated in the media. It is, of course, part of the wider collective social ideal of Black men—big, strong, powerful, fast, and scary. There is, of course, some truth to this, but we devalue the true varied talents of an individual when we collectively limit them to such tropes. I can't recall how many times I've heard a commentator refer to Black players with the old adage *power and pace, or call them a beast*. Paul Pogba is a very good modern-day example of this, an amazingly gifted footballer who is often reduced to his physical and athletic attributes. Pogba is not only a World Cup winner, but he is also one of the best technicians in the game and someone who excels in the aforementioned roles that are often ring-fenced from Black players. Yaya Touré is another great example of this—a tall, physically imposing Black player who is technically extremely gifted but usually highlighted for his physicality alone.

The opposite side of this is also true for those Black players who are less physically imposing in terms of size. N'Golo Kanté is a good example of this. He is one of the best defensive midfielders of the modern era, having won multiple Premier League titles, a World Cup, and a Champions League trophy. He was man of the match for most of the Champions League winning run, no small feat for an important, but sometimes overlooked, position. His position on the pitch ironically is largely about *positioning*, that is to say, reading the game and having a high degree of mental acumen. Kanté is also a great athlete, although in this instance more in regard to his stamina. He is often lauded for his 'engine' i.e. his stamina rather than the mental side of his game that makes him one of the best; this is not a position you can bluff on physicality alone.

The media portrayal of Black footballers was pointedly encapsulated by ex-manager Ron Atkinson, who famously described Black player Marcel Desailly as 'A fucking lazy thick nigger'.[231] What is particularly interesting about this incident was not just the overtly disgusting racism that he unintentionally broadcast on air, but that Ron Atkinson is someone who could be considered as kind of a pioneer because he was one of the first managers to select Black players in the '70s. This is exactly why it's so interesting; Ron is one of the 'good guys' and look at what is running around in his head about Black players, so you can only imagine what other people are thinking.

This positioning of Black men is not accidental. Overtly or not, it is about maintaining a narrative of brute force that is dehumanising. We are not allowed to be masters of guile, intellect, or craft; we have to be kept to the realms of the physical alone. And heaven forbid should we embrace both… that, of course, would be truly frightening. The idea that Black athletes are not up to par mentally is something that feeds heavily into the off-the-field challenges.

Representation Off the Field

There are many US sports where Black people dominate the playing squads and other sports like football (soccer) where they represent a significant part of the teams in the West. Despite the high prevalence and contribution on the field, there is a clear lack of representation.

If we look at the US, we see that the NBA is made up of about 75% African American players while only 23% of the 30 teams had Black head coaches in the 2020–2021 season and only 1 majority owner.[232] The NFL is in a similar situation where you have a majority of African American players at ~70% but only 1 head coach/manager and 0 African American owners.[233]

This is a similar situation with EX US football (soccer), where there are usually around 5 managers of colour occupying any of the 92 professional football teams, only 7 in 2021, around 7%.[234] This is clearly disproportional when we look at the players of colour across the league—around 25%.

Even sporting legends are not seemingly able to transcend this glass ceiling. The great Michael Jordan, a man often compared to God, such was his basketball prowess, winner of 6 NBA rings, 5-time MVP, 10-time leading scorer, All-Star team regular, and 2-time Olympic Gold medal winner, to name a few of his achievements. World-renowned as the greatest basketball player of all time, at the end of Jordan's playing career, he was offered a role as the team president for the Washington Wizards. This was to be Jordan's transition from player to the upper echelons of the NBA business world. The front office business role for the Wizards team, something that very few African American players manage to occupy, a just reward for the greatest ever basketball player of all time, who, in addition, was the basis for Nike's brand Jordan and the multiple billions generated.

Shortly after starting as team president, Jordan decided to re-join the playing staff to help the team. When Jordan joined the team, they were $40 million in debt. His decision to play again was responsible for selling out every one of the 82 regular home season games, generating $30 million. At the end of the season when Jordan expected to return to his role as team president, he was asked to leave. The greatest player of all time was discarded as cheaply as yesterday's newspaper because he was no longer useful. His role and primary value were on the court and the financial revenue his name could generate through marketing and sales. When that was no longer on offer, he was no longer needed. Jordan, it was said, had finally found out what it meant to be African American. It is worth noting that this did not stop Jordan from pursuing his dreams for ownership as he went on to become majority owner of the Charlotte Bobcats.

Making Things Better

Collective and sanctioned protest and significant punishment

For significant improvements in terms of addressing racism at sporting events by fans or players, there are a couple of channels that need to be addressed. The first is the collective support of players of all races, managers, fans, and supporting staff, supporting Black players facing abuse in the game and their decision to stop playing if they see fit. From other players on the team, this could mean refusing to play on in support of their teammate. From fans, it should mean condemning other fans who participate in racial abuse. Everyone should be aligned against racism and make it clear that it is more important than any game. In 2020, for the first time ever, we saw NBA players and, because of enough collective support, teams refusing to play play-off matches in protest against police brutality following the shooting of unarmed Black man Jacob Blake who was shot seven times in his back in front of his family and left paralysed.

Continuing with sporting protests and uprisings in the US, we also saw another first with NFL players taking the knee during a game, only a few short years after Colin Kaepernick was blackballed from the game for peacefully protesting in exactly the same way.

Broader representation across clubs and organisations...

The second channel is at the level of sporting governing bodies. In an attempt to level the playing field and correct for the disproportionate representation of people of colour with corrective legislation. The first example is the 2003 Rooney Rule—the National Football League (NFL) policy that required all teams to interview ethnic minority candidates for head coaching and senior operation jobs. There is no requirement to hire anybody, only to interview.

Since the Rooney Rule was established, several NFL franchises have hired African American head coaches, including the Pittsburgh Steelers themselves who hired Mike Tomlin before their 2007 season. At the start of the 2006 season, the overall percentage of African American coaches had jumped to 22%, up from 6% prior to the Rooney Rule.[235]

In the next 12 seasons under the rule, the NFL added 14 non-White head coaches, although many lost their jobs after a few seasons. For the 2019 season, eight NFL teams had head coaching vacancies to fill, but only one team, the Miami Dolphins, hired a non-White coach. As of 2020, the NFL has three African American head coaches, the same number as in 2003 when the Rooney Rule was first adopted, suggesting limited long-term progress.[236]

In US college basketball, we saw the introduction of the Russell Rule in August 2020, which requires each member institution of the West Coast Conference of teams to include a member of an under-represented community in the pool of final candidates for every athletic director, senior administrator, head coach, and full-time assistant coach position in the athletic department.[237]

FA diversity codes

The UK Football Association (FA) have announced diversity codes to help combat discrimination and systemic barriers in the UK game. The *codes* are guidelines that will help increase representation in coaching and executive roles from BAME (Black and minority ethnic) backgrounds and women.[238]

For those who may not know, you see a clear disparity in football in the amount of BAME players compared to off-the-field roles like coaching or executive management. Looking at English football today, we see that only five of the 92 Premier League and English Football League (EFL) clubs have managers or head coaches that are BAME. That is around 5%, compared with around 20% of BAME players that are in the game—a clear mismatch. It is worth noting that not only are BAME players representing around 1 in 5 of all players, they make up significant proportion of the best players in the game today e.g. Pogba, Rashford, Aubameyang, Son, Salah, and Mane (current PFA fans player of the year), just to name a few.

What do the codes look like?

- 15% of new executive appointments will be from a BAME background, with 30% women.

- 25% of new coaching appointments will be BAME and 10% of senior coaching appointments.
- 50% of new coaching appointments at women's football clubs will be female, with 15% BAME.
- Shortlists for interview will have at least one male and one female BAME candidate, provided applicants meeting the job specifications apply.

Ex-professional Paul Elliott, head of the FA Inclusion Advisory Board, says the new code will 'hold football to account'. 19 of the 20 Premier League clubs have agreed to the voluntary code so far, with Southampton the only exception. Southampton have said they are 'wholly supportive' of the code's objectives but are waiting to see how it fits in with the Premier League's own Advanced Equality Standard before revising their recruitment processes, which they say are the culmination of a 'five-year equality and diversity journey.'

Social media IDs to combat online racism

As the fight continues against racism, we do not have to look hard to find very present reminders of how much work needs to be done, with regular occurrences of discrimination in all walks of society. An area that is especially visible is the online abuse suffered by high-profile people of colour, particularly football players. In the past few years, we have seen Manchester United players Anthony Martial, Eric Bailly, and Marcus Rashford, Chelsea player Reece James, Manchester City's Raheem Sterling, Arsenal's Bukayo Saka, and many others suffer racial abuse online.

Of course, this is nothing new and has been going on in football stands from fans towards players of colour for decades; this online version is just an extension of that. What is perhaps most attractive to bigots about online abuse is the anonymity afforded by the internet and social media platforms. Just create a dummy account and be free to say whatever you want without repercussions. This problem of cloaked racism has led to the suggestion that social media IDs or passports should be created where an individual account could be traced back to a real person.

Would social media IDs be a good idea?

On the positive side, they would help prevent this type of racism and make it easier for people to be held accountable. The average person has their account linked to their e-mail address; it wouldn't be much of an extra burden to add your passport number to your login. However, the argument against this measure is that it would constitute an increase in surveillance culture, something that is already on the rise and could threaten our civil liberties.

I think social media platforms need to work harder to prevent online abuse by issuing lifetime bans and reporting people to the police who breach the rules of racism and other forms of discrimination. I believe it is important to share these instances to spread awareness of how often these attacks take place. However, I understand that it can be draining to constantly have to deal with abuse, and people may not want to share every instance of racism they encounter; as Black people, we know that we would not get much else done. It is up to the individual to do what they think is best.

As a community—fans, players, managers—we can also do more to condemn individuals who are racist online and of course in wider society.

Increased ownership and management

Connected to increased representation at different levels of sporting organisations off the field is a focus on the executive suite, in particular ownership. Ownership is of pivotal importance because it facilitates autonomy and decision-making. Ownership by individuals truly invested in the interests of the Black community will enable the best chance of fairer representation off the field. There are so many examples across different sectors of minority business owners, particularly South Asians who employ people from their own community. It is not a necessity, but it does give you the power to do so, should you choose.

The Interconnectedness of Sport

The issues we see in sports concerning barriers to entry based on race and lack of representation in off-the-field positions of influence are similar to those observed in other entertainment worlds and across the job market in general. Indeed, the lack of ownership and executive control in fields where we are integral are key economic challenges, as discussed earlier. The more pronounced issue of fields that are dominated by or have significant contributions from people of colour, like the NBA or hip-hop, while having limited representation at ownership, management and executive levels is particularly problematic. More work needs to be done to increase representation in these positions so that more favourable directions can be made to fight against discrimination, protect those who speak out and benefit economically from all the talent and hard work we are putting into the respective fields of play. The racial abuse endured by so many players is, of course, not limited to sporting arenas but a form of abuse that most Black people face in their daily lives; stressors and traumas that can impact our mental health, as we will discuss next.

Chapter 9: Psychological and Mental Health

'Imperialism leaves behind germs of rot which we must clinically detect and remove from our land but from our minds as well.'[239]
– Frantz Fanon

In this chapter:

Challenges

- Mental health: direct and indirect race-based stressors
- Racism and psychological safety
- Psychological impacts: insecurity and overcompensation
- Psychological impact: self-hate and stigma

Making things better

- Increasing access to mental health care
- De-stigmatising mental health in the community
- Creating psychologically safe spaces

We have discussed the barrage of information that creates a near constant onslaught on the senses in terms of media messaging and environment. If we tie together the threads of music, entertainment, and beauty standards, coupled with the historic prejudices that are still very present today, as well as the very real economic and legislative structural barriers in place, we have a significant attack on the psyche.

A rarely asked question is, what is the psychological impact of all these strenuous factors? After hundreds of years of bondage, segregation, and discrimination, is there a mental impact? I would argue, yes. In fact, with so much trauma, I think it would be strange if there wasn't. In effect, mental conditioning is taking place from birth, with direct and indirect messages and narratives being communicated on a daily basis. What are the mental consequences of being regularly subjected to racial discrimination, being oppressed by various systemic structures, witnessing police officers murder people in your community and escape without any punishment… living in a world without justice?

In addition to the challenges of direct and indirect racial trauma, there are other contributing factors, such as poverty and homelessness that increase the chance of the Black community developing mental health issues. I want to discuss a few areas where we see this phenomenon manifesting. Adult African Americans are 20% more likely to present with serious psychological distress than White Americans.[240]

It has been established that stress and trauma can lead to psychological damage and mental health problems. Experiencing racism in both explicit and implicit ways is stressful, and traumatic experiences can directly impact our mental health and psychological state. This logical path needs to be explored in more detail, but looking at some of the evidence, we see that there is a clear problem.

Explicit Racism and Mental Health

Mental health

Mental health discussions, in general, have only recently started to rise to prominence in public discussion, and in the Black community, this lack of attention is even greater. We will go on to review some of the prevalent flags of mental health within the Black community, where we see higher levels than in other groups. In addition, it is important to understand some of the drivers for the phenomena that are taking place e.g. direct and indirect experiences of racism, socioeconomic factors such as poverty, homelessness, and living in violent neighbourhoods, increased incarceration, and internalisation of negative narratives. Much more research is needed as this is an under-investigated area, but the weight of the findings to date is alarming.

A summary from UK charity MentalHealth.org highlights that people from BAME are 'more likely to be diagnosed with mental health problems, more likely to be diagnosed and admitted to hospital, more likely to experience a poor outcome from treatment, more likely to disengage from mainstream mental health services.'[241]

As mentioned, there are external drivers for mental health issues in the community e.g. racism, poverty, and being subjected to negative narratives, and there are some internal problems e.g. stigma within the community. I will begin with the external factors...

Direct experience of racism (direct traumatic stressors)

Direct traumatic stressors include all specific experiences that impact someone's life. For example, this may include traumatic experiences from living within a society that is structurally racist like being stopped and searched by the police because of your skin colour or being on the receiving end of a racial slur.

Indirect experience of racism (vicarious traumatic stressors)

Vicarious traumatic stressors are indirect traumatic experiences that occur from living in a racist environment. For example, watching Black men and women get slaughtered by the police on camera—George Floyd, Philando Castile, Tamir Rice, to name a few. It is thought that these indirect examples of trauma can be just as mentally damaging as direct examples of trauma.

Socioeconomic factors – poverty, homelessness, and violent neighbourhood

In addition to the daily direct experiences and indirect vicarious experiences, there are also socioeconomic factors that play a role in the psychological well-being and mental health of people of colour. People of colour are often living in poorer communities and have lower socioeconomic status.

Coming from this type of environment usually means high exposure to more stressful circumstances e.g. worrying about money for food or bills and usually poorer access to healthcare, particularly mental healthcare. Black people are three times more likely to be homeless in the US. Moreover, minorities represent 39% of homeless people and only 13% of the total population.[242] While in the US, in 2020, African Americans account for double the poverty level: 20% that of White poverty levels of around 8%.[21] Adult African Americans living below the poverty line are twice as likely to report serious psychological distress than those living above it.[243]

The mental strain of (mass) incarceration

We have discussed mass incarceration in the US, people of colour account for 38% of the US prison population, while making up only around 13% of the US.[244] Unfortunately, incarceration levels for the Diaspora across the West are also disproportionately high. It doesn't take much imagination to understand that prison is a very stressful environment. There is a lot of data that shows the deteriorating impact prison can have on people mentally; this is unsurprising when we consider how dangerous and frightening prison can be—a place where your life can literally be at risk. The Institute of Psychiatry estimates that half of prisoners have poor mental health, including depression, PTSD, and anxiety.[245] The relatively high number of people in the community who endure these experiences adds to the collective burden of mental and psychological illness within the community.

Mental health statistics for the Diaspora: What are the impacts of these traumatic stressors on mental health?

In terms of mental health prevalence in the UK, we see that:

- Afro-Caribbean people are 3 to 5 times more likely to be admitted to hospital for schizophrenia.[246]
- Black men experience psychosis 10 times more often than White men.[247]
- Black adults have the lowest treatment rates for mental health: 6.2% vs. 13% for White people.[248]
- Afro-Caribbean men are at an increased risk of suicide.[249]
- Afro-Caribbean men are 1.5 times as likely to present with PTSD.[250]
- The 2014 Adult Psychiatric Morbidity Survey (APMS) found the prevalence of common mental health problems to vary significantly by ethnic group for women, but not for men. Non-British White women were the least likely to have a common mental health problem (15.6%), followed by White British women (20.9%) and Black and Black British women (29.3%).[251]

The policing of Black people with mental illnesses also paints a concerning picture:

- Disproportionate rates of people from BAME populations have been detained under the Mental Health Act 1983. Black people were four times as likely to be detained compared to White people.[252] A 2016 UK study examining the Mental Health Act 2007 found that Black people have disproportionally higher rates of mental health conditions and poorer levels of social support, but not due to ethnicity.[253]

- People of colour are more likely to be obligated to receive mental health treatment through the courts and police, instead of receiving voluntary treatment.[247]
- Black people are more likely to be designated a medium or high-security risk.[247]

The picture across the pond seems to be slightly better, but problems are still prevalent, particularly in terms of access to care and suicide rates:

- Only one in three African Americans who need mental health care receives it.[254]
- The type of care received is also of concern. African Americans have lower rates of outpatient service use, including prescription medications, but higher use of inpatient services,[255] suggesting African Americans are presenting at a later more serious stage and/or they are being treated more forcefully when they encounter the health system.

The mental health picture appears to be better in the US, with rates of serious mental health similar between different demographics at around 12%.[243] However, it is worth noting that suicide is the second biggest killer of younger African

Americans (15–24), with men at four times greater risk than women.[243]

The impact of implicit racism on mental health and psychological safety/health

The strain on mental health and psychological safety (feeling free to be your true self with full acceptance and at no detrimental cost) is not always driven by lower socioeconomic conditions or overt acts of racism. What can be even more common is relatively 'small' daily acts of racism. These remarks may seem insignificant but experienced frequently add up – and have an impact, something akin to death by a thousand cuts.

Implicit Psychological Threats:

Microaggressions and subconscious bias

Microaggressions and subconscious bias are two examples of threats to psychological safety that are often experienced by people of colour. These are potentially daily events that we have been wrongly conditioned to normalise and accept. Microaggressions describe relatively small or subtle acts that may not be intended to be aggressive but actually have a harmful impact. An example of a microaggression is being in an elevator and clutching your bag because you are scared of a person of colour who is sharing the same space. Many of these microaggressions and subconscious/implicit/unconscious biases are based on the negative stereotypes that have been crafted e.g. the criminal Black male or strong Black woman that we discussed earlier.

Interestingly, there are some 'bias masking' experiments that have taken place, which show the true subconscious feelings of fear held by some White people. The amygdala is part of the brain that is associated with fear and other emotions. It has evolved from what is called the reptilian part of the brain, one of the oldest areas, which is integral to survival tactics. This part of the brain was monitored after being shown Black faces at a subliminal speed, too fast to consciously process. After seeing these faces, White people exhibit more aggression in various contexts. In addition, in an association test, White people more frequently associated negative words e.g. terrible, failure, horrible, evil, agony, war, nasty, and awful with Black faces compared to White faces. Professor Brian Nosek ran an experiment with over 700,000 subjects and found that more than 70% of White subjects more easily associated White faces with positive words and Black faces with negative words.[256] Moreover, experiments have shown that this conditioning is not limited to White people; Black people also show the same discrimination against ourselves. Microaggressions also manifest as questions or statements. While some are deliberately triggering, there are also instances where unwitting subconscious biases are at play. Here are some examples of microaggressions:

'All lives matter.'

This is a common response to Black Lives Matter, usually from people who are unsympathetic to the ongoing oppression of Black people. Aside from the obvious nature of the statement, it is a subversive way of suggesting that the lives of Black people should not receive special attention. Your struggle is not important because other people struggle too. This flawed logic is akin to having a broken arm and the doctor telling you all bones matter, instead of helping you fix your broken arm. Interestingly and perhaps in slightly poor taste, the hashtag #allbuildingsmatter trended on 9/11 in 2020, referring to the tragic events of the Twin Towers falling. This tongue-in-cheek approach flips the all lives matter logic on its head, suggesting that 9/11 does not merit special attention and remembrance when all buildings are of equal importance. It clearly articulates the point.

'I have a Black friend.'

The notion of someone somehow being exempt from the possibility of being racist because they happen to have one or maybe a few Black friends is seriously flawed. As we have seen with the rise in interest in the Black struggle, for example with the attention initially generated by the BLM movement, many White people are not well-educated on the subject. Somewhat admirably, there has been an outcry for information and support on how to be an ally. So clearly, there can be people who mean well but perhaps through their own ignorance are still acting offensively. You could have a Black friend and still ask to touch their hair, for example. Racism isn't as simple as not using the N word or not partaking in lynching; it is complex and nuanced. True allies will seek to learn and grow, not exempt themselves from the conversation under the presumption that they have all the answers.

'Can I touch your hair?'

Speaking of hair, can I touch yours? No. Emma Dabiri, the academic and author who wrote the brilliant book *Don't Touch My Hair,* which explores in detail many of the problems associated with White control of Black hair. From what is considered professional, i.e. natural afro hair being considered messy or unprofessional, while Prime Minister Boris Johnson is at liberty not to groom at all, to invasively overstepping personal boundaries and inviting themselves to experience a personal part of the body, something that is sacred to most Black women.

'Where are you from? No, where are you really from?'

This query may seem innocent on the surface, and again, sometimes the intention may well be, but the impact and effect may not be. The problem with the question is when somebody White is trying to understand the 'deeper' roots of your ethnic background under the proviso that people that look like you are not from the West. This strips a person of their choice to be associated with a country they were likely born in. I know people who have parents from parts of the world that they have never been to. Are they from those places? On further inspection, the idea that people of colour cannot claim the West as their place of origin, even if that's where they landed on Earth, is flawed. People of colour have been in these countries for hundreds of years and some would say longer, and I think more importantly, looking at the sacrifices people of colour have made for these countries, e.g.

African Americans, they are more than entitled to claim that place as home, should they so choose.

'You're smart for a Black guy. You're very well spoken.'

Here, again, the implication is that the standard of higher education is White and that Black people typically attain below that standard. I have a BSc and a Master's in Neuroscience from two of the best universities in the UK. I still see the shock on people's faces at times when they hear what I've studied. An interesting thing about that reaction is that it is subconscious, ingrained, and even automatic to a degree because they have been programmed to think that way—Black people aren't scientists. A permutation of this is being congratulated on your command of the English language. Again, there is surprise in the fact that you are so well-spoken; that isn't the expectation of a person of colour. The preconceptions of society are that you speak slang or that you will have a limited vocabulary. Let's be clear, I've had people go as far as to say, 'You speak White.'

'You are pretty…for a Black girl.'

This comment harks back to the Western beauty standard narrative and, sadly, is not only delivered by White people; there are also people of colour who have been conditioned to think that Western beauty standards are the ideal. The implication that non-Western Black beauty is less than, so if you somehow manage to have Black skin but still fall in the parameters of Western beauty e.g. straight hair or a thin nose then you deserve a compliment is self-hate at its finest. If you are a White person who shares that sentiment, then you are simply racist.

'I never owned slaves.'

Here is a funny one, 'I've never owned slaves'. The logic of this argument is that genuine racism only happened in the past and a long-distance past. Contemporary reality is fair and said person has never acted in a discriminatory way. A problem with this view is that it shows a lack of understanding of the challenges of racism, clearly that racism is just a thing of the past, and that they have such nuanced present-day understanding of the Black experience that they have never ever acted in a way that perpetuates White privilege, never made an unintentionally hurtful comment (like this one). The person who makes this type of statement is actually invariably more likely to be racist because of the crude way they view racism.

'I can't believe that happened.'

This signal of intended support can often be frustrating because it feeds into the idea that the experience you've endured is somehow unbelievable as if to say that it is actually unlikely that things played out that way. This is particularly annoying because it is probably something you've experienced often e.g. someone holding their bag when they are with you in the lift—this happens **ALL** the time. I don't want to be harsh on people who mean well; as mentioned, this is supposed to be a supportive statement, but it can have a detrimental effect.

Many of these microaggressions and subconscious/implicit/unconscious biases are based on the negative stereotypes that have been crafted e.g. the criminal Black male or strong Black woman that we discussed earlier. Having to endure these types of comments is just one example of the psychological drain placed on the psyche of Black people every day.

These are just the supposedly smaller and less significant examples of racism that add stress to our lives. This is not remarking on the major overt stressors like explicit racism e.g. being verbally or physically assaulted because of your race or witnessing racism.

Internalised Impact

Living While Black

The phrase 'Living While Black' describes the burden of the everyday Black experience in the West. This ranges from the most stark and offensive encounters of racism to the most subtle instances of microaggression. For me, it encapsulates the constant background level of near subconscious tension and alertness that many people in the Diaspora carry around with them on a daily basis, things that we have been conditioned to internalise, often unknowingly. At times, I try to reflect on behaviours that I have internalised without realising to allow me to more comfortably fit into the world around me, from writing off verbal abuse in public as an unusual occurrence, 'a bad apple', to making myself as small and unthreatening as possible when in tight spaces like a lift with White people to thinking carefully about what clothes I wear. Working in a corporate environment, my office attire is smart shoes, trousers, and a shirt, all very 'presentable'; this version of me is received much more positively by general (White) society than me in my casual outfits of tracksuit bottoms and trainers, which became much more common for most of us during lockdown and working from home. Of course, it is far less problematic for a White guy to walk around in a hoody and other forms of comfortable clothing than it is for a Black man. In addition to the encounters of racism I've experienced, growing up in London, my friends and I have been denied entry to bars and clubs because we were Black. These are all examples of things that we in the Diaspora have learned to minimise and accept as part of 'normal' life, 'not that big of a deal'. But the truth is it is a big deal and it all adds up; these are added stressors and pressures that collate, on top of the general weight of life, to lead to the mental health disparities that were discussed earlier.

There psychological burden of living in a racist world, experiencing these microaggressions and other discriminatory stressors can have some devastating internal psychological impacts. Not only can they lead to direct health issues, but they can also drive unhealthy behaviour and narratives.

Insecurity issues and overcompensation

One clear example of the psychological impact of centuries of subjugation and poverty is the seemingly implicit desire to overcompensate. The compulsion to show off material wealth is all too prevalent among many members of the African Diaspora. When people 'make it' there is usually a compulsion to buy fancy things, from jewellery to cars and clothes. No doubt, this is heavily driven by a psychological reaction responding to a life of poverty. There are definitely poor people from other communities who get a bit excessive when they come into money, but this overt response appears to be more pronounced in the Black community. Diamond-encrusted rappers, the bling lifestyle, and the epitome of excess are synonymous with newly rich Black folk. Youngsters posing on Instagram with 'money phones' (a large stack of cash pressed to one's ear like a phone) are all typical exploits of the nouveau riche. Ironically, this extreme showmanship comes across more like the performance of a minstrel than anything else.

An American sales video from the 1950s aptly illustrates the understanding of African American buying behaviour at the time. The 'training' video runs a simulation of a shop environment where Black consumers are highlighted as being the group most likely to spend large sums of money on goods that will depreciate (lose value over time), e.g. clothes. Shop assistants are trained to look out for the Black consumer and target them for an easier sell. Fast forward 50 or so years and this dynamic remains. 'High fashion' designers e.g. the Guccis and Fendis of the world know that the Black community, poor or rich, will clamour to be draped in their garb, ultimately as a sign of success and, I believe, on a more subconscious level to fill a void of self-worth.

What is particularly sad about the situation with the luxury fashion houses is they are so confident of the business they will get from the Black community; they make no effort to cater to us. In fact, on multiple occasions, we have seen these fashion houses be overtly racist, as seen with Moncler's Black face jacket incident, safe in the knowledge that irrespective of how badly we are treated, we are psychologically damaged enough to come back for more. I don't want to be too judgmental about a time when people of African descent were actively told they were, and forced to be, less than other members of society; centuries of being put down is going to have an impact, but we need to do better.

In a world that tells that you are less than, you are a suspect, a criminal, less important, the desire to try and buy a sense of self-worth seems like a logical move. I've arrived. I can do as I please and the life I've spent not being recognised ends here. You will acknowledge me through my wealth.

Self-hate/self-destruction

Self-hate is a relatively broad and perhaps somewhat abstract term, but in this instance, it refers to a mental state of being that facilitates self-destructive behaviour. This self-hate can manifest consciously or subconsciously and can be identified in some of the examples from the previous chapter around negative narratives that are being internalised and brought to life in a self-destructive way.

Let's take gang violence as an example. We know that this violence within a community is heavily driven by poverty and proximity. However, we have to also accept that the negative narratives in some forms of hip-hop, trap and drill music, where artists are clearly promoting murder and violence is in some way responsible for the violence that we see amongst the same Black men who consume (and perform) this type of music. The level of violent messaging towards people within our own community is not the same as in other poorer communities. You do not hear Bangladeshi music talking about killing other Bangladeshi people exclusively. We have to ask why this is so unique to ours. We also have to ask why the aim and target of our frustration is within the community mainly, compared to a police force that we know will harass the community with stop and search and worse in the UK and regularly murder in the US. Or more music targeted at a government system that allows this system to remain in place.

Part of the problem, of course, is the motives of record labels and what they want to promote. But the challenge is, why are we not asking these questions of ourselves more broadly and challenging these realities? That is on us. We also touched on the perceived Western beauty standard in the previous chapter. With particular reference to skin bleaching, here we see the clear psychological damage of colourism resulting in the literal self-destruction of one's skin to appear fairer.

As discussed previously, this mentality is crucial to facilitating Black-on-Black violence and self-destructive behaviour.

Although thankfully less common these days, self-hate can also manifest as an overt desire to assimilate and be accepted by Western culture. Don't get me wrong, there is nothing wrong with adopting or embracing aspects of the country you live in or were raised in. I am instead referring to the denial or rejection of aspects of ourselves that are connected with being people of colour. Historically, this would have been things like 'conking' our natural curly hair with harmful chemicals, so it becomes straight and 'White-looking'. This may also be seen with a fear of wearing our hair natural today, or avoiding certain styles like braids or locs, for fear of judgement. Sadly, I've experienced more; I had a person of colour (in Switzerland) tell me to 'not tan too much' on holiday, and risk getting 'too dark'. This was a semi-joke, with a large amount of sincerity, from someone who had grown up in an environment where he learned to hate his brown complexion.

Improvements Needed from Within the Community

There are also internal challenges that need to be faced that contribute to the problem of mental health in the community.

Fear of engagement with services, disproportionate sectioning, and distrust of medical professionals

Black people are more likely to enter the mental health system through the courts and not via a GP or other health practitioner. We are also significantly more likely to be sectioned under the Mental Health Act and are more likely to receive medication instead of behavioural therapies.

Related to the previous point is also the issue of distrust of medical professionals in general. In the medical and health section, we covered some of the reasons why the Black community would not trust medical professionals. This distrust can lead to lower recognition of developing mental health conditions because people are less inclined to go and visit a specialist.

Negative stigma associated with mental health

In some parts of the community, there is still an old-fashioned and unhelpful negative stigma around mental health. It is seen as a sign of weakness and having internalised the idea that we should not be and cannot be weak. This again leads to denial, lower recognition and lower diagnosis. A study demonstrated that 63% of African Americans considered mental health issues to be a sign of personal weakness.[254] It's great to see more celebrities and 'role models' like UK rappers Dave and Stormzy talking openly about their own personal struggles with mental health. The more people discuss and normalise mental challenges that are common for many of those in society, particularly those in the limelight, the more we can destigmatise the topic and enable more people to confront what they may be going through and seek help.

Lack of minority professionals leading to a lack of connection, rapport, and enthusiasm to seek treatment

As with other areas of health, the Black community is under-represented. Mental health is a particularly sensitive topic, unlike other areas of health, being treated by someone who has a better chance of understanding your experience i.e. someone from your background is very important. For example, it would be harder to discuss the traumatic racism you've experienced with someone who is from the very community causing the stress. Likewise, it is also difficult to expect that person to understand such experiences that they could never experience. The fact that there is a low chance of being treated by someone from your community is an added barrier to wanting to seek treatment.

Transgenerational transmission of trauma through family, etc. (RES)

Lastly, there is the very sensitive topic of transgenerational transmission of trauma, something that I think is very significant in the Black community. We have experienced so much pain for so long, passing on this pain is almost unavoidable—pain from father to son, mother to daughter...

Further Research

Like in the world of physical health and medicine, people from the Diaspora are under-represented in the world of mental health and psychological research, particularly in terms of the mental strain caused by living in racist environments. The sample sizes are small and are often not specific to those from the Black community but broader minority communities. This lack of research is a significant problem as it is hard to quantify the scale of the problems people are facing without it. We know people in the Diaspora are subject to many different types of mental stressors and triggers, but in terms of impact, the best we can do is look at the prevalence rate for certain conditions. I know that many people in the Diaspora are forced to internalise and suppress the daily challenges they face in the hope of just carrying on.

Studies show that Black and minority populations are under-represented in mental health research.[257] A few reasons have been cited for this: investigators running studies may prefer homogenous groups so as to reduce any confounding results that could be created by different groups. Black people have less access to mental healthcare and these care services are often pools for study recruitment.

As mentioned, there is some resistance in the community to volunteer for studies, somewhat linked to community narratives that should be challenged but also because there is a lack of trust and an unhealthy relationship with those in positions of power—as we know minorities are forcibly detained at a higher proportion than Whites. MQ is a mental health research organisation that has recognised the under-representation of Black people in this particular area of research. Through the charity, you can donate funds to help facilitate further research into the community. This under-representation not only means that we do not know enough about the experience and realities of mental health in people of colour, but it also means that practitioners are not well-equipped to treat us.

A paper in *Lancet Psychiatry* suggests that some of the challenges facing the Black community in this field, for example being sectioned at a higher rate, are actually because of this lack of understanding:

> *the cultural distance between White Western European psychiatrists and Black men, which has led to the medical profession being out of touch with the reality of this community's experiences. The authors stated that it had contributed to Black and minority ethnic minority groups being twice as likely to be misdiagnosed and subjected to*

an inappropriate service-led approach to their mental health needs in Britain.[258]

Making Things Better

In the area of mental health and psychology, solutions or paths forward are particularly hard to identify because these topics are so complicated, even before you consider the compounding impact of racial discrimination or socioeconomics, but here are some ideas:

Decreasing race-based trauma

Clearly decreasing the chance of experiencing race-based trauma will have a beneficial impact. By removing or decreasing the stressors caused by direct and indirect racist events, we can create a less stressful environment that is conducive to better mental health. A couple of ways we can achieve this is through education to avoid accidental traumatic events and tougher punishments to deter deliberate traumatic events.

Care and socioeconomics

The data shows that people of colour are not receiving adequate care, in effect being failed by the system. Improvements need to be made to ensure that ethnicity is not a barrier to receiving appropriate care. We also know that there needs to be more mental health professionals from minority backgrounds who will be better placed to understand the challenges faced by someone in a minority. Less than 2% of American Psychological Association members are African

American. This is exacerbated by the fact that some African American patients report experiencing racism and microaggression from their own therapists.

In addition, linked to the socioeconomic arguments discussed earlier, there is a clear imperative to raise the economic base and lift more people out of poverty so they can access better care and treatment. This is a similar sentiment for healthcare in general. Alternatively, more programs could be funded to provide better healthcare treatment to the poorest and most vulnerable members of our society.

There are some organisations that specialise in providing care for Black people, for example, Black Minds Matter in the UK can connect families with Black therapists for free,[259] while the Black, African and Asian Therapist Network has a directory of therapists from these backgrounds.[260] In the US, there are multiple organisations that serve African Americans; for example, BEAM (Black Emotional and Mental Health) provides training and grants and is dedicated to the wellness of the Black community.[261] Therapy for Black Girls is an online platform dedicated to the mental well-being of Black women.[262]

De-stigmatisation of mental health

Growing up, I remember how the term 'mental' was thrown around as an insult. 'You're mental', someone would say, meaning you were 'crazy'. Reflecting on those days, I can see that there was a lot of innocence and ignorance attached to the jibe based on a sheer lack of understanding and the impetuousness of youth. Unfortunately, moving into adult life within the Black community and wider society at large, the ignorant comment evolved into a more significant negative stigma around mental health—the idea that if you suffer from a mental health condition that something is really wrong with you; it is somehow abnormal compared to a more general health issue such as cancer. This stigma means that people are less likely to try and recognise potential problems for fear of the shame of being labelled mentally unwell. We need to actively promote the importance of mental health, encouraging people to share and discuss problems in safe spaces, but also combat the shame and stigma. Suffering from a mental health condition or being depressed is not abnormal; on the contrary, it's increasingly common.

We are starting to see more high-profile people, e.g. celebrities like Stormzy and Dave, publicly address mental health in their music and also openly discuss the challenges they've faced. UK rapper Dave's first studio album was titled *Psycho*, with several tracks tackling the issue of mental health and shining a light on the topic. Footballer Danny Rose has also spoken up about the mental health challenges he's faced. These awareness-raising actions can help to normalise the issue for people and remove the stigma, providing a clearer path to better mental health.

Psychologically safe environments

Creating a more psychologically safe society is generally important, a world where people can be comfortable being themselves, free from judgment or persecution based on their race, sexual orientation, religion, or any other life choice that does not harm others. In the workplace, this can be addressed with training to make people aware of how comments, that may seem innocent, can be negatively interpreted e.g. 'Where are you from?' Surveys can be conducted to assess the level of safety employees think they have e.g. do they feel safe to raise a concern with management, challenger safety, and contributor safety.[263]

In terms of bringing your 'authentic self' to work or school, i.e. who you truly are as a person, without intrinsic corporate or vocational adjustments. It is about ensuring that the respective working environment is safe to do so; e.g., Can you wear your natural hair? e.g. the Halo Code, a guide for schools and workplaces to prevent discrimination around hairstyles or texture. The co-founder of the Halo Code is 16-year-old Katiann Rocha who had experienced racist comments about the condition of her hair being called 'messy' or 'unkept'. Around 30 people are involved with the code, and the guidelines have already been adopted by the large conglomerate Unilever.

- Protection: If you are a person of colour with afro hair that isn't straightened or short enough to conform to Western beauty standards, it is not uncommon to be challenged on your hairstyle and pressured to change it. This is a form of oppression and racism. There are a few particularly high-profile cases of school children sent home from school because their hair is 'too big' (Ruby Williams) or banned from school because of wearing dreadlocks (12-year-old Chikayzea Flanders, Fulham Boys School), but it's a common theme. We also know that many women of colour straighten their hair in order to assimilate more easily in the workplace. This code is important to have the necessary protection against persecution for something as natural and personal as our hair.

- Freedom of expression and cultural identity: Unlike many other cultures, afro hair has strong cultural roots and messages. On a more superficial but still important level, we use our hair as an expression of who we are, whether it's afro, fade, or braids, it sends a message about how we want to be seen as people. We take great pride in our hair, spending hours and relatively large amounts of money to have it styled in a way we like. The barbershop for Black men is a haven. Having a new trim for a Black man has a level of personal significance greater than most other ethnicities.

- More importantly, it is more about our cultural heritage rather than just the way we happen to wear our hair. Its unique range of textures allows us to style in ways that other people cannot replicate. The very texture we are often taught to hate is the base of the beauty we create. In addition, a deeper look into our history shows that our hairstyles have been the basis of early demonstrations of fractals, binary codes, and maps to communicate routes to freedom during slavery.

- Casual racism with broader implications: Commenting on hair and controlling it is an example of insidious casual racism: what might seem a small act on the surface is very significant. The command to change your natural being into something more acceptable to White society is in effect White supremacy. 'Your hair is different to mine; mine is the standard and yours is lower. I do not want to have to experience your hair—remove it'. You are being forced into submission and altered to be more palatable to Western norms. It is through acts of supremacy like this that you stifle and replace cultural identity, just like during slavery when indigenous language was removed, history erased, and deities replaced.

The US has their own version of the Halo Code called the CROWN Act. The CROWN Act, which stands for Create a Respectful and Open World for Natural Hair, is a law that prohibits race-based hair discrimination, which is the denial of employment and educational opportunities because of hair texture or protective hairstyles including braids, locs, twists, or Bantu knots.[264] As of March 2022, this law has been passed in 14 states, with 36 to go. The picture of discrimination based on the natural hair of Black people is a clear one. A study from the CROWN Act organisation shows:[264]

- 53% of Black mothers, whose daughters have experienced hair discrimination, say their daughters have experienced race-based hair discrimination as early as 5 years old.
- 86% of Black teens who experience discrimination state they experienced discrimination based on their hair by the age of 12.
- 100% of Black elementary school girls in majority-White schools who report experiencing hair bias and discrimination state they experienced the discrimination by the age of 10.

Psychological safety is very important to our mental health and sense of belonging. We cannot be at peace mentally or feel like we are truly part of a school or organisation if we do not have this safety. I grew locs whilst working in a corporate environment with the knowledge that this could isolate me. However, it was more important for me to be true to myself than to acquiesce for the sake of acceptance.

Self-care

In a world that is increasingly asking more of us, physically and mentally, we all need to prioritise self-care. That includes ensuring you're living a healthy lifestyle: balanced diet, exercise, and rest, to name a few. In terms of mental health that also includes being aware of your mental state. Are you feeling okay? Are you stressed? Run down? Ensuring you proactively discuss and try to address any stresses you may experience, seek help, meditate, and don't let the problem linger. Are you in an environment that is causing you stress? Do you have relationships that are negatively impacting your mental health? Perhaps you need to address the problems you have with a person to improve the situation.

The Interconnectedness of Mental Health and Psychology

The issues faced with mental health and the psychological strains of being part of the African Diaspora in the West are intrinsically connected to other areas discussed in this book. We see differences in treatment as we do in other areas of health. We see the disproportionate use of stricter measures such as sectioning, as we do with sentencing in the traditional justice system. The burdens of lower socioeconomic status create stressors that can become drivers for the mental health issues faced by the Diaspora. Negative narratives of violence and materialism that are promoted in music and media can be internalised and drive us to undertake self-destructive behaviour and to seek self-worth in material items. These behaviours are primarily psychological in origin. We also observe a need for greater narrative control to reinforce our self-worth in order to combat the barrage of psychological stressors, from microaggressions through to the mental toll of direct and indirect racial trauma.

Chapter 10: In Closing

'Education is the most powerful weapon which you can use to change the world.'[265]
– Nelson Mandela

The aim of this book was to provide an overview of the different challenges faced by the African Diaspora, their interconnected nature, and suggest some potential paths forward. If it wasn't clear before reading, I hope it is now that there are many barriers and forms of racial discrimination in practically all walks of life. The breadth and depth of the problems facing the Diaspora may seem overwhelming, but progress has been made and can continue. On the bright side, there is much more that can be done to improve things.

We have discussed key problems across many areas of life from the historical impacts of bondage to the economic challenges that face the community, through to the socioeconomic barriers that are in place, as well as more ephemeral and psychological problems, media representation, negative narratives, and images of perceived beauty. Within all these problems, there are consistent themes of White supremacy, exploitation, disparities and oppression. Racism is a societal ill that is truly ubiquitous and pervasive, a tinted lens that shapes the world for all those who look through it. From doctors and judges to mortgage lenders and football coaches, the story is a similar one. Of course, not every White person is racist or shares the same level of unconscious bias, but the historic foundations are rooted so deep, the present-day reality is so stark, that any White person who is genuinely against racism should reflect deeply—not only within themselves but also interrogating the world around them.

The challenges faced have, for the most part, been created by others, but are not solely theirs to own. I believe in agency and empowerment, and fortunately, there are significant improvements that can be made from within, especially tackling self-created or self-perpetuated issues e.g. challenging the stigma around mental health or overtly promoting negative narratives amongst our community through our music and other media.

The Interconnectedness of Things

A key part of understanding the challenges we face in the Diaspora is the interconnected nature of the problems. The issues described in this book are not unconnected. Understanding the bigger picture and the related nature of the issues is important to forming solutions. We cannot look at mass incarceration and the prison-industrial complex and ignore the negative narratives pushed through the media that contribute to it. We cannot fully understand and face the challenges of lack of ownership in areas we dominate without understanding the broader economic landscape and changes that are needed. We cannot increase our own knowledge of self and self-worth without challenging the educational barriers that are in place. It is important to identify issues of historical legacy that impact our present-day reality, from being experimented on while in bondage to disparities in maternal death rates.

Completing the Loop and Broader Responsibilities

For those who manage to transcend difficult circumstances and manage to make it to some form of independence and 'freedom', there is an implicit duty to give back, sharing what we've learned and helping others to also transcend. Key to this is an understanding that economic growth and political *freedom* are not enough. Generating wealth for yourself and your family should not be the summit; we all have to work together to uplift each other. An individualistic view of success is not the best outcome; this will only lead to limited progression. We need to have a broader community and global view—not just limited to the individual challenges faced in the West by members of the Diaspora.

The problem with individual success alone in the West

From Obama to the smattering of Black people who make it to executive levels or senior roles in companies, there are stories of individual success in the Diaspora. Financially too, particularly in the world of sports and entertainment, there are plenty of examples of successful and relatively wealthy people of colour. These examples are often lauded as proof that problems of systemic or interpersonal discrimination are not so bad.

Despite these success stories from the few, we know that many remain in more difficult circumstances at the bottom of most indexes from poverty to health and beyond. I believe a more conscious decision has to be made to not focus on individual achievement and maintaining the status quo, but instead think more collectively to have a larger positive impact on the community. After all, how much genuine satisfaction is there in being surrounded by wealth while the rest of your people are struggling? When we look at the speed the Black dollar or Black pound leaves the community, and the lack of group economics and collective community initiatives, it is clear to see that much more could be done.

A more global view

Beyond the borders of the UK, US, and other Western countries, there are those who need support at home in Africa and the Caribbean. In many ways, liberation for the Diaspora in the West is contingent on success at home—what many would consider their true home. Despite the fractured nature of some relationships between those in the Diaspora and their home nations, these connections are key.

While it is important to fight for better conditions in the Western countries that have become our more recent homes, the speed of change would be significantly faster with stronger African and Caribbean home nations. This is exemplified by how other groups e.g. Asians are treated in the US. An anti-Asian hate bill was passed very quickly in the US, while African Americans only just received an antilynching bill in 2022, after years of campaigning—the Bill that makes race-based lynching a hate crime was rejected almost 200 times.[266] It finally passed despite three Republicans still voting against it. This is not a coincidence. International power and pressure count for a lot. There is no way police brutality would be allowed to impact Asian communities the way in which it does African Americans and Black Brits.

Finding ways to build bridges with the 'motherland', replenishing the brain drain that has taken place and helping to build those developing economies is an important goal, not only for a better experience in the West but also for the implicit duty of developing our true homes. In analogous terms, I often think, can a man or woman who does not take care of their family ever be truly respected?

Reasons for Optimism

Despite the challenges we face, there are genuine reasons to be optimistic. The challenges are all surmountable, and we have seen and will continue to see great examples of success against the odds. Our challenges should be acknowledged appropriately but with the primary objective of how to transcend, not to be hindered by them. The shackles that can be consciously or subconsciously placed on people because of circumstance, history, and environment are dangerous if people feel helpless. On the contrary, we are seeing numerous examples of excellence within the Diaspora and paths to overcome the hurdles that are in place. We need to eradicate any semblance of blame culture and become self-determining.

Self-love and self-worth

We need to work on our core foundation, and everything starts with you; it begins with loving yourself. You need to love yourself enough to want a good life for yourself. You need to love yourself enough to value your life and not be willing to lose it to crime or violence. Part of the journey is based on knowing who you are and understanding your history, knowing you are more than just a descendant of slavery. You need to truly believe you deserve a good life free from persecution and full of opportunity.

Self-love is critical to beating the narratives in play that communicate you are less than that you're not beautiful enough or smart enough or creative enough to succeed. This is imperative to get out of the tight boxes we are currently confined to. You can do anything—if you want to be an entrepreneur in green energy, you can do it. We are not limited to sports and entertainment (although we are, of course, pretty good at those things).

Community

Part of the journey is a great sense of community, looking to help others and not just ourselves. Seeing people who look like you and going through the same challenges as you are—not as threats but rather as collaborators and support.

A community view will influence how you are choosing to conduct yourself. How are you making your money? Is it to the detriment of others? What is the potential impact of that song? Are you uplifting? These are the questions we need to ask ourselves.

Greater economic independence

A solid economic foundation is a route to overcoming a lot of the socioeconomic barriers that blight the community. Everything from the allure of criminal life and poorer housing to underfunded education and lower quality healthcare. These things can be significantly improved with greater resources. We need to become economically savvier, make better use of our money, keep it circulating in the community for longer, diversify our revenue streams, and gain more ownership of the industries we dominate and the things we create. Part of this is ensuring we are represented in a wider range of fields, especially those in the private sector and the industries of the future, especially in the field of technology.

Change from within

Many people will be pessimistic about internal change occurring in the political and legal system. However, I think this is the most pragmatic approach. Increasing representation of people who genuinely care and want to make a difference, people who can put the issues of people of colour on the agenda and achieve policy change, and fighting for programmes like the EMA are important. Of equal if not greater importance is voting and participating in elections *en masse* so we have some democratic weight to bargain with. It is unlikely that a political party is going to take any interest in a demographic that does not contribute a significant number of votes.

A brighter future

It would be unjust to suggest that the problems that face those in the Diaspora are small or insignificant. I have tried to take the time to outline what I consider to be the most problematic issues in a pragmatic way. Increasingly militarised police forces that use excessive levels of force against those in the Diaspora from Brazil to Boston to Birmingham is a real issue. The level of underfunded public services that disproportionately impact those of colour is a real issue. The growing prison-industrial complex and mass incarceration are real issues. However, the key takeaway of this book is that there is hope and there is opportunity.

There is no better time in history than now to succeed. We have a solid foundation in terms of civil liberties and freedoms that previous generations have fought so hard to win. We also have technological advances and opportunities that previous generations did not have. The online potential and social media channels provide vast opportunities to create businesses and define our own narratives—Instagram channels like Black British Parent, Black Business Review, The Black Young Professionals Network, Black Pound Day, and the plethora of pages on 'Black Twitter' and other social media platforms. As we continue to make progress, we have greater cause for hope that we will achieve what we need to.

Epilogue

It's a Wednesday afternoon. I'm in the office getting ready to connect with my Diversity and Inclusion colleagues about one of our workstreams looking at how we can help tackle health disparity. As we brainstorm ideas around improving access to treatments for disadvantaged communities and improving clinical trial representation, a bird lands on a branch outside the window, catching my attention. I begin to mentally drift and reflect on the changes in the world over the last few years, changes sparked largely by the brutal murder of George Floyd and the subsequent new-found energy individuals and major corporations had for the Black struggle. How pledges and promises were made; how more and more people were speaking up. I felt a sense of optimism, that finally out of all the darkness, some light was coming through. For the first time in Western history, all areas of society were actively listening to the concerns of people of colour and other minorities. There is opportunity for change.

As my mind continues to wander, I consider a future state for the African Diaspora, for the world. Quality education is available to everyone. Those in Black communities are not restricted to dangerous neighbourhoods. We in the Diaspora showcase our talents across varied sectors, free to authentically present as ourselves. We are no longer targeted by law enforcement or subject to low-quality healthcare. We see broader and more positive stories in our media outlets. Sportspeople can play without fear of racial abuse. Our economic foundation is strong and mental health in good stead...

A colleague brings me back to reality for the start of the meeting...

***

This book has taken me about five years to write, most definitely a labour of love, with as much enjoyment as frustration. My mindset has taken a positive trajectory from when I began writing to ''t generations have had to endure. They will be equipped with the tools to make the necessary change.

Finally, I continue to see Black excellence on a daily basis, whether it's a show like Michaela Coel's *I May Destroy You*, a film like *Malcolm & Marie,* or amazing technological advances like British-Ghanaian Danny Manu who developed earbuds that can automatically translate 40 languages. It's everywhere and growing every day, but we cannot afford to let up and release the pressure. We need to continue to push and strive for more to ensure we create a better world for future generations.

Recommended Reading

- *How Europe Underdeveloped Africa* – Walter Rodney
- *The Mis-Education of the Negro* – Carter G. Woodson
- *The New Jim Crow* – Michelle Alexander
- *Black Skin, White Masks* – Frantz Fanon
- *When We Ruled* – Robin Walker
- *Natives: Race and Class in the Ruins of Empire* – Akala
- *White Fragility* – Robin DiAngelo
- *Don't Touch My Hair* – Emma Dabiri
- *The Good Immigrant* – Various authors
- *Black and British: A Forgotten History* – David Olusoga
- *Brit(ish)* – Afua Hirsch
- *The COINTELPRO Papers* – Ward Churchill
- *Morning in South Africa* – John Campbell
- *The Rise and Fall of Black Wall $treet* – Robin Walker
- *Up from Slavery* – Booker T. Washington
- *The Souls of Black Folk* – W.E.B. Du Bois

- *The Autobiography of Malcolm X* – Malcolm X and Alex Haley
- *Medical Apartheid* – Harriet A. Washington
- *The Color of Money* – Mehrsa Baradaran
- *Forty Million Dollar Enslaved people* – William C. Rhoden
- *The Spook Who Sat by the Door* – Sam Greenlee
- *Women, Race and Class* – Angela Davis
- *Nice Racism* – Robin Di Angelo

References

[1] 'What caused the 1985 Tottenham Broadwater Farm riot?' (2014) *BBC News,*
https://www.bbc.co.uk/news/uk-england-london-26362633

[2] Mohdin, A. and Murray, J. (2021) ''The Mark Duggan case was a catalyst': the 2011 England riots 10 years on', *The Guardian,*
https://www.theguardian.com/uk-news/2021/jul/30/2011-uk-riots-mark-duggan#:~:text=On%204%20August%202011,engulfed%20by%20fire%20and%20violence

[3] 'Stephen Lawrence murder: A timeline of how the story unfolded' (2018) *BBC News,*
https://www.bbc.co.uk/news/uk-26465916

[4] 'George Floyd: Timeline of black deaths and protests' (2021) *BBC News,* https://www.bbc.co.uk/news/world-us-canada-52905408

[5] Garvey, M. (1991) *The Marcus Garvey and Universal Negro Improvement Association Papers*. Berkeley, California: The University of California Press, p. 204.

[6] Bacon, F. (1597) *Meditationes Sacrae*.

[7] Du Bois, W.E.B. (1903) *The Souls of Black People*.

[8] Percheski, C. and Gibson-Davis, C. (2020) A Penny on the Dollar: Racial Inequalities in Wealth among Households with Children, *Socius: Sociological Research for a Dynamic World,* 6.

[9] Toby Helm, (2016) 'Brexit camp abandons £350m-a-week NHS funding pledge'. *The Guardian*, https://www.theguardian.com/politics/2016/sep/10/brexit-camp-abandons-350-million-pound-nhs-pledge

[10] Heinlein, R. A. (1987) *Time Enough for Love*, London: Penguin, p. 223.

[11] Martin Luther King Jr.

[12] 'Lynching from 1882–1968', *NACCP,* https://naacp.org/find-resources/history-explained/history-lynching-america

[13] 'The Origins of Modern Day Policing', *NACCP,* https://naacp.org/find-resources/history-explained/origins-modern-day-policing

[14] Henry Louis Gates, Jr., 'The Truth Behind '40 Acres and a Mule'', *PBS*, https://www.pbs.org/wnet/african-americans-many-rivers-to-cross/history/the-truth-behind-40-acres-and-a-mule/

[15] 'The Haitian Revolution', *Britannica*, https://www.britannica.com/place/Haiti/The-Haitian-Revolution

[16] Daut, M. (2020) 'When France extorted Haiti — the greatest heist in history', *The Conversation*, https://theconversation.com/when-france-extorted-haiti-the-greatest-heist-in-history-137949

[17] 'Sharecropping' (2010) *History* https://www.history.com/topics/Black-history/sharecropping

[18] 'Education during the slave period in the United States', *Wikipedia*, https://en.wikipedia.org/wiki/Education_during_the_slave_period_in_the_United_States

[19] Tyler Cowen

[20] Madam C.J. Walker

[21] 'Poverty rate in the United States in 2021, by ethnic group' (2021) *Statista* https://www.statista.com/statistics/200476/us-poverty-rate-by-ethnic-group/

[22] Haider, A., 'The Basic Facts About Children in Poverty', American progress.org
https://www.americanprogress.org/article/basic-facts-children-poverty/

[23] Wilson, V. (2020) 'Racial disparities in income and poverty remain largely unchanged amid strong income growth in 2019', *Economic Policy Institute.*
https://www.epi.org/blog/racial-disparities-in-income-and-poverty-remain-largely-unchanged-amid-strong-income-growth-in-2019/

[24] McIntosh, K., Moss, E., Nunn, R., and Shambaugh, J.(2020) *Examining the Black-white wealth gap*, Brookings.edu
https://www.brookings.edu/blog/up-front/2020/02/27/examining-the-Black-White-wealth-gap/

[25] US Census Government Data
http://pubdb3.census.gov/macro/032005/hhinc/new05_000.htm

[26] Passy, J. (2020) 'Black homeownership has declined since 2012 — here's where Black households are most likely to be homeowners', *MarketWatch*,
https://www.marketwatch.com/story/black-homeownership-has-declined-since-2012-heres-where-black-households-are-most-likely-to-be-homeowners-2020-06-30

[27] Asante-Muhammad, D., Buell, J., and Devine, J. (2021) '60% Black Homeownership: A Radical Goal for Black Wealth Development', *National Community Reinvestment Coalition,*
https://ncrc.org/60-Black-homeownership-a-radical-goal-for-Black-wealth-development/

[28] National Low Income Housing Coalition (2013) 'Report Shows African Americans Lost Half Their Wealth Due to Housing Crisis and Unemployment National Low Income Housing Coalition'
https://nlihc.org/resource/report-shows-african-americans-lost-half-their-wealth-due-housing-crisis-and-unemployment

[29] 'The Economic State of Black America 2020', *Joint Economic Committee Democrats*,
https://www.jec.senate.gov/public/index.cfm/democrats/2020/2/economic-state-of-Black-america-2020

[30] 'Income distribution', Gov.uk.
https://www.ethnicity-facts-figures.service.gov.uk/work-pay-and-benefits/pay-and-income/income-distribution/latest

[31] Fain, K. (2017) 'The Devastation of Black Wall Street', *JSTOR Daily,*
https://daily.jstor.org/the-devastation-of-Black-wall-street/

[32] Little, B. (2020)'How a New Deal Housing Program Enforced Segregation', History.com
https://www.history.com/news/housing-segregation-new-deal-program#:~:text=Roosevelt%20established%20to%20stimulate%20the,backing%20of%20loans%E2%80%94guaranteeing%20mortgages.

[33] Baradaran M. (2017) *The Color of Money: Black Banks and the Racial Wealth Gap.* Boston: Harvard University Press.

[34] Frey, W. H. (2018) 'Black-White segregation edges downward since 2000, census shows', Brookings.edu https://www.brookings.edu/blog/the-avenue/2018/12/17/Black-White-segregation-edges-downward-since-2000-census-shows/

[35] Perry, A. M., Rothwell, J., Harshbarger, D. (2018) 'The devaluation of assets in Black neighborhoods', Brookings.edu. https://www.brookings.edu/research/devaluation-of-assets-in-Black-neighborhoods/

[36] Bayer, P., Fernando Ferreira & Ross, S. L. (2016) *What Drives Racial and Ethnic Differences in High Cost Mortgages? The Role of High Risk Lenders*, National Bureau of Economic Research (NBER).
https://www.nber.org/papers/w22004

[37] Passy, J. (2021) 'Black homeownership rate hits lowest level since the 1960s — that's unlikely to change in Pandemic Year 2', MarketWatch.com.
https://www.marketwatch.com/story/most-Black-americans-arent-homeowners-how-can-we-change-that-11615431459

[38] Jan, T. (2017) 'Here's why the wealth gap is widening between White families and everyone else', *The Washington Post*.
https://www.washingtonpost.com/news/wonk/wp/2017/10/05/heres-why-the-wealth-gap-is-widening-between-White-families-and-everyone-else/

[39] Moore, A., and Bruenig, M. (2017) 'Without the Family Car Black Wealth Barely Exists', People's Policy Project.org.

https://www.peoplespolicyproject.org/2017/09/30/without-the-family-car-Black-wealth-barely-exists/

[40] Darity, W., and Mullen, K., (2020)
'Black reparations and the racial wealth gap', Brookings.edu.
https://www.brookings.edu/blog/up-front/2020/06/15/Black-reparations-and-the-racial-wealth-gap/

[41] 'Frequently Asked Questions About Small Business' (2020)
https://cdn.advocacy.sba.gov/wp-content/uploads/2020/11/05122043/Small-Business-FAQ-2020.pdf

[42] Cassandra West, 'Building Black-owned bigger', *Crain's Chicago Business*.
https://www.chicagobusiness.com/equity/chicagos-Black-owned-businesses-look-scale

[43] Austin, A. (2016) 'The Racial Gap In Entrepreneurship Is Costing The U.S. Economy Billions', *IMDiversity*,
https://imdiversity.com/diversity-news/the-racial-gap-in-entrepreneurship-is-costing-the-u-s-economy-billions/

[44] Austin, A. (2016) *The Color of Entrepreneurship: Why the Racial Gap among Firms Costs the U.S. Billions*.

[45] Brooks, R.A. (2020) 'More than half of Black-owned businesses may not survive COVID-19', *National Geographic*.
https://www.nationalgeographic.com/history/article/Black-owned-businesses-may-not-survive-covid-193

[46] McKinsey Institute for Black Economic Mobility (2020) 'Building supportive ecosystems for Black-owned US businesses', *McKinsey & Company,* https://www.mckinsey.com/industries/public-and-social-sector/our-insights/building-supportive-ecosystems-for-Black-owned-us-businesses

[47] Davies, N. 'Black-Owned Businesses Are Still Struggling to Find Investors', *Crunchbase,* https://about.crunchbase.com/blog/Black-owned-businesses-are-still-struggling-to-find-investors/

[48] 'Race in the workplace: The Black experience in the US private sector' (2021) *McKinsey & Company,* https://www.mckinsey.com/featured-insights/diversity-and-inclusion/race-in-the-workplace-the-Black-experience-in-the-us-private-sector

[49] 'Employment by sector' (2022) Gov.uk. https://www.ethnicity-facts-figures.service.gov.uk/work-pay-and-benefits/employment/employment-by-sector/latest

[50] Makortoff, K., 'UK Black professional representation 'has barely budged since 2014', (2020) *The Guardian,* https://www.theguardian.com/business/2020/jun/22/uk-Black-professional-representation-has-barely-budged-since-2014

[51] 'Race and ethnicity in the NBA', *Wikipedia.* https://en.wikipedia.org/wiki/Race_and_ethnicity_in_the_NBA

[52] 'The First Black American Becomes Owner of a Major American Sports Franchise', https://aaregistry.org/story/first-Black-owner-of-a-major-sports-franchise/

[53] 'Share of players in the NFL in 2020, by ethnicity', *Statista*. https://www.statista.com/statistics/1167935/racial-diversity-nfl-players/

[54] 'Black H Regimens Boost Shampoo Sales in the US to Reach $473 Million in 2017' (2017) *Mintel*, https://www.mintel.com/press-centre/beauty-and-personal-care/Black-haircare-regimens-boost-shampoo-sales-in-the-us

[55] 'Black Impact: Consumer Categories Where African Americans Move Markets' (2018) *Nielsen*, https://www.nielsen.com/us/en/insights/news/2018/Black-impact-consumer-categories-where-african-americans-move-markets.html

[56] Owen, L. H. (2016) 'A Howard project is debunking myths about African-Americans and teaching students fact-checking', NiemanLab. https://www.niemanlab.org/2016/01/a-howard-project-is-debunking-myths-about-african-americans-and-teaching-students-fact-checking/

[57] The Village Market, https://thevillagemarketatl.com/about-the-village/

[58] Help to Buy: Equity Loan, Gov.uk, https://www.gov.uk/help-to-buy-equity-loan

[59] Black Young Professionals Network, https://byp-network.com/

[60] BlackPages UK, https://www.Blackpagesuk.com/

[61] Black Pound Day, https://Blackpoundday.uk/

[62] Barton, L. L. (2021) 'What It's Like to Be a Black Man in Tech', *Harvard Business Review*. https://hbr.org/2021/03/what-its-like-to-be-a-Black-man-in-tech

[63] Ekeke, O. (2021) 'Tackling tech's big diversity problem starts with education', *WIRED*, https://www.wired.co.uk/article/racial-equality-tech

[64] Lago, C. (2020) 'Black representation in tech: What the figures don't tell us', *Tech Monitor*, https://techmonitor.ai/leadership/workforce/Black-representation-tech-what-figures-dont-tell

[65] Schnuer, J. (2021) 'Greenwood, the mobile banking app founded by Andrew Young and Killer Mike, wants to help Black communities build generational wealth', *Fortune*, https://fortune.com/2021/12/01/killer-mike-andrew-young-greenwood-banking-app-Black-communities-generational-wealth/

[66] 'Stormzy Scholarship for Black UK Students', The University of Cambridge, https://www.undergraduate.study.cam.ac.uk/stormzy-scholarship

[67] Reed, R. (2019) '21 Savage Expands Financial Literacy Campaign, Pledges Money to Atlanta Youth', *Rolling Stone*, https://www.rollingstone.com/music/music-news/21-savage-financial-literacy-campaign-atlanta-812779/

[68] Blay, Z. (2019) 'Nipsey Hussle's Work in The Black Community Went Deeper Than You Think', *HuffPost*, https://www.huffingtonpost.co.uk/entry/nipsey-hussle-Black-community-activism_n_5ca4ba20e4b0798240256d96

[69] The Data Team (2018) 'The stark relationship between income inequality and crime', *The Economist*, https://www.economist.com/graphic-detail/2018/06/07/the-stark-relationship-between-income-inequality-and-crime

[70] Fajnzylber, P., Lederman, D., and Loayza, N. (2001) 'Inequality and Violent Crime', *The Journal of Law and Economics*, 45(1), https://web.worldbank.org/archive/website01241/WEB/IMAGES/INEQUALI.PDF

[71] Mayor of London (2019) 'Full links between poverty and violent crime in London', Mayor of London, https://www.london.gov.uk/press-releases/mayoral/full-links-between-poverty-and-violent-crime

[72] Becker, G. (2011) *Crime and Punishment: An Economic Approach.* https://sites.duke.edu/econ206_01_s2011/files/2015/03/Becker_CrimePunishment_TeamGrossmanHandout.pdf

[73] Santacreu, A. M. and Zhu, H. (2017) 'How Does U.S. Income Inequality Compare Worldwide?', Federal Reserve Bank of St Louis, https://www.stlouisfed.org/on-the-economy/2017/october/how-us-income-inequality-compare-worldwide

[74] Statista Research Department (2023) 'Countries with the largest number of prisoners as of July 2021', *Statista*, https://www.statista.com/statistics/262961/countries-with-the-most-prisoners/

[75] 'Public Housing: Image Versus Facts' (1995) HUD.gov, https://www.huduser.gov/periodicals/ushmc/spring95/spring95.html#:~:text=Forty%2Deight%20percent%20of%20public,percent%20of%20all%20renter%20households.

[76] Reschovsky, A. (2017) 'The Future of U.S. Public School Revenue from the Property Tax', Linconlist.edu., https://www.lincolninst.edu/sites/default/files/pubfiles/future-us-public-school-revenue-policy-brief_0.pdf

[77] Morgan, P. (2009) 'Risk Factors for Learning-Related Behavior Problems at 24 Months of Age: Population-Based Estimates', *Journal of Abnormal Child Psychology,* 37(3), 401-413, https://www.ncbi.nlm.nih.gov/pmc/articles/PMC3085132/

[78] Hackman, D. A., Farah, M. J., and. Meaney, M. J., (2010) 'Socioeconomic status and the brain: mechanistic insights from human and animal research', *Nature Reviews Neuroscience*, 11(9), 651-659, https://www.ncbi.nlm.nih.gov/pmc/articles/PMC2950073/

[79] Goodman, A., and Gregg, P. (2010) *Poorer children's educational attainment: how important are attitudes and behaviour?* Joseph Rowntree Foundation. https://www.jrf.org.uk/sites/default/files/jrf/migrated/files/poorer-children-education-full.pdf

[80] 'Education and Socioeconomic Status', American Psychological Association, https://www.apa.org/pi/ses/resources/publications/education

[81] 'Education and Socioeconomic status', American Psychological Association, https://www.apa.org/pi/ses/resources/publications/factsheet-education.pdf

[82] McFarland, J., Cui, J., and Stark, P. (2018) 'Trends in High School Dropout and Completion Rates in the United States: 2014', National Centre for Educational Statistics, https://nces.ed.gov/pubs2018/2018117.pdf

[83] Timpson, E. (2019) *Timpson Review of School Exclusion* https://assets.publishing.service.gov.uk/government/uploads/system/uploads/attachment_data/file/807862/Timpson_review.pdf

[84] McIntyre, N., Parveen, N., and Thoma, T. (2021) 'Exclusion rates five times higher for Black Caribbean pupils in parts of England, *The Guardian*, https://www.theguardian.com/education/2021/mar/24/exclusion-rates-Black-caribbean-pupils-england

[85] Tinson, A. (2020) 'Living in poverty was bad for your health long before Covid-19', *The Health Foundation*, https://www.health.org.uk/publications/long-reads/living-in-poverty-was-bad-for-your-health-long-before-COVID-19

[86] Taylor, J. (2019) 'Racism, Inequality, and Health Care for African Americans', The Century Foundation. https://tcf.org/content/report/racism-inequality-health-care-african-americans/?agreed=1

[87] Artiga, S., and Hill, L. (2022) 'Health Coverage by Race and Ethnicity, 2010–2019', KFF, https://www.kff.org/racial-equity-and-health-policy/issue-brief/health-coverage-by-race-and-ethnicity/

[88] Lackland, D. T. (2014) 'Racial Differences in Hypertension: Implications for High Blood Pressure Management', *The American Journal of the Medical Sciences August 2014*, 348(2), 135–138, https://www.ncbi.nlm.nih.gov/pmc/articles/PMC4108512/

[89] King, C. J., Moreno, J., Coleman, S. V., and Williams, J. F. (2018) 'Diabetes mortality rates among African Americans: A descriptive analysis pre and post Medicaid expansion', *Preventive Medicine Reports,* 12, 20-24, https://www.ncbi.nlm.nih.gov/pmc/articles/PMC6097282/#:~:text=There%20was%20a%20slight%20reduction,an%20increase%20of%209.53%2F100%2C000.

[90] Strait, J. E. (2021) 'Triple-negative breast cancer more deadly for African American women', Washington University School of Medicine in St Louis, https://medicine.wustl.edu/news/triple-negative-breast-cancer-more-deadly-for-african-american-women/#:~:text=Among%20women%20with%20triple%2Dnegative,chemotherapy%20among%20African%20American%20patients.

[91] 'African Americans and Prostate Cancer', Zero Cancer. https://zerocancer.org/learn/about-prostate-cancer/risks/african-americans-prostate-cancer/

[92] Croxford, R. (2020) 'Coronavirus: Black African deaths three times higher than White Britons — study', *BBC News,* https://www.bbc.co.uk/news/uk-52492662

[93] Census 2021 (2020)'Why have Black and South Asian people been hit hardest by COVID-19?' Office of National Statistics, https://www.ons.gov.uk/peoplepopulationandcommunity/healthandsocialcare/conditionsanddiseases/articles/whyhaveBlackandsouthasianpeoplebeenhithardestbycovid19/2020-12-14

[94] Gawthrop, E. (2023) 'The Color of Coronavirus: COVID-19 Deaths by Race and Ethnicity in the U.S.', APM Research Lab. https://www.apmresearchlab.org/covid/deaths-by-race

[95] Baldwin, J. (1962) 'AS MUCH TRUTH AS ONE CAN BEAR; To Speak Out About the World as It Is, Says James Baldwin, Is the Writer's Job As Much of the Truth as One Can Bear', *New York Times*, January 14, 1962.
https://www.nytimes.com/1962/01/14/archives/as-much-truth-as-one-can-bear-to-speak-out-about-the-world-as-it-is.html

[96] Washington, H.A. (2007) *Medical Apartheid*. he Dark History of Medical Experimentation on Black Americans from Colonial Times to the Present, New York: Doubleday

[97] Holland, B. (2017) ''The 'Father of Modern Gynecology' Performed Shocking Experiments on Enslaved Women', https://www.history.com/news/the-father-of-modern-gynecology-performed-shocking-experiments-on-enslaved people

[98] Nix, E. (2023) 'Tuskegee Experiment: The Infamous Syphilis Study', History.com.
https://www.history.com/news/the-infamous-40-year-tuskegee-study

[99] Racism and Research: The Case of the Tuskegee Syphilis Study, Havard.edu.
https://dash.harvard.edu/bitstream/handle/1/3372911/Brandt_Racism.pdf?sequence=1&isAllowed=y

[100] Cohen, S. A. (2008) 'Abortion and Women of Color: The Bigger Picture', *Guttmacher Policy Review*, 11(3), https://www.guttmacher.org/gpr/2008/08/abortion-and-women-color-bigger-picture

[101] 'Our History, Planned Parenthood', Planned Parenthood, https://www.plannedparenthood.org/about-us/who-we-are/our-history

[102] Hawkins, K. (2020) 'Remove statues of Margaret Sanger, Planned Parenthood founder tied to eugenics and racism', *USA Today*, https://eu.usatoday.com/story/opinion/2020/07/23/racism-eugenics-margaret-sanger-deserves-no-honors-column/5480192002/

[103] Parker, S., and Dannenfelser, M. (2022) 'The Impact of Abortion on the Black Community', CurePolicy.org. https://curepolicy.org/report/the-impact-of-abortion-on-the-Black-community/

[104] 'The Human Genome Project', National Human Genome Research Institute. https://www.genome.gov/human-genome-project#:~:text=Beginning%20on%20October%201%2C%201990,for%20building%20a%20human%20being.

[105] McKay, R. R., Gold, T., Zarif, J. C., Chowdhury-Paulino, I. M., Friedant, A. Gerke, T., Grant, M., Hawthorne, K., Heath, E., Huang, F. W., Jackson, M. D., Mahal, B., Ogbeide, O., Paich, K., Ragin, C., Rencsok, E. M., Simmons, S., Yates, C. Vinson, J., Kantoff, P. W., George, D. J., and Mucci, L. A. (2021) 'Tackling Diversity in Prostate Cancer Clinical Trials: A Report from the Diversity Working Group of the IRONMAN Registry', *JCO Global Oncology*, 7, 495-505, https://ascopubs.org/doi/full/10.1200/go.20.00571

[106] DePolo, J. (2021) 'Triple-Negative Breast Cancer Deadlier for Black Women, Partially Due to Lower Surgery, Chemotherapy Rates', BreastCancer.org, https://www.breastcancer.org/research-news/triple-negative-breast-cancer-deadlier-for-Black-women

[107] Siddharth, S., and Sharma, D. (2018) 'Racial Disparity and Triple-Negative Breast Cancer in African-American Women: A Multifaceted Affair between Obesity, Biology, and Socioeconomic Determinants', 10(12), 514, https://www.ncbi.nlm.nih.gov/pmc/articles/PMC6316530/

[108] Reid, S., Kennedy, L., Mayer, I., and Pal, T. (2021) 'Addressing Racial Disparities in Breast Cancer Clinical Trial Enrollment', *ASCO Daily News*, https://dailynews.ascopubs.org/do/10.1200/ADN.21.200499/full/

[109] GWAS Diversity Monitor, https://gwasdiversitymonitor.com/

[110] The King's Fund (2012/13) 'Demography: Future Trends', *The King's Fund Analysis of Office for National Statistics 2010-based National Population Projections*, The King's Fund, https://www.kingsfund.org.uk/projects/time-think-differently/trends-demography

[111] World Health Organization (2019) 'Building regional bridges to strengthen and promote civil society NCD coalitions in Francophone sub-Saharan Africa', https://ncdalliance.org/news-events/news/building-regional-bridges-to-strengthen-and-promote-civil-society-ncd-coalitions-in-francophone-sub-saharan-africa

[112] World Health Organization (2022) Cancer Key Statistics https://www.who.int/cancer/resources/keyfacts/en/

[113] Keogh-Brown, M. Jensen, H. T., Arrighi, H. M., and Smith, R. D. (2016) 'The Impact of Alzheimer's Disease on the Chinese Economy', 4, 184-190, https://www.sciencedirect.com/science/article/pii/S2352396415302474

[114] Vidyasagar, D. (2005) 'Global notes: the 10/90 gap disparities in global health research', *Journal of Perinatology*, 26, 55–56, https://www.nature.com/articles/7211402

[115] Farooq, F., Mogayzel, P.J., and Lanzkron, S. (2020) 'Comparison of US Federal and Foundation Funding of Research for Sickle Cell Disease and Cystic Fibrosis and Factors Associated with Research Productivity', *JAMA Network Open*, 3(3), e201737, https://jamanetwork.com/journals/jamanetworkopen/fullarticle/2763606

[116] The Associated Press (2021)'NFL agrees to end race-based brain testing in $1B settlement on concussions', *NPR*, https://www.npr.org/2021/10/20/1047793751/nfl-concussion-settlement-race-norming-cte?t=1645613797315

[117] Sabin, J.A. (2020) 'How we fail Black patients in pain', *AAMC*, https://www.aamc.org/news-insights/how-we-fail-Black-patients-pain

[118] Elahi, A. S. (2021) 'Covid: Pulse oxygen monitors work less well on darker skin, experts say', *BBC News*, https://www.bbc.co.uk/news/health-58032842

[119] U.S. Department of Health and Human Services (2019) 'Racial and Ethnic Disparities Continue in Pregnancy-Related Deaths', *CDC Newsroom*, https://www.cdc.gov/media/releases/2019/p0905-racial-ethnic-disparities-pregnancy-deaths.html

[120] 'Pregnancy Mortality Surveillance System' (2023) CDC, https://www.cdc.gov/reproductivehealth/maternal-mortality/pregnancy-mortality-surveillance-system.htm

[121] Flanders-Stepans, M. B. (2000) 'Alarming Racial Differences in Maternal Mortality', *Journal of Perinatal Education*, 9(2): 50-51, https://www.ncbi.nlm.nih.gov/pmc/articles/PMC1595019/

[122] Novoa, C., and Taylor, J. (2018) 'Exploring African Americans' High Maternal and Infant Death Rates', American Progress.org.

https://www.americanprogress.org/article/exploring-african-americans-high-maternal-infant-death-rates/

[123] Anekwe, L. (2020) 'Ethnic disparities in maternal care', *BMJ*, 368: m442.
https://www.bmj.com/content/368/bmj.m442

[124] Summers, H. (2021) 'Black women in the UK four times more likely to die in pregnancy or childbirth', *The Guardian*, https://www.theguardian.com/global-development/2021/jan/15/Black-women-in-the-uk-four-times-more-likely-to-die-in-pregnancy-or-childbirth

[125] Howell, E. A. (2018) 'Reducing Disparities in Severe Maternal Morbidity and Mortality', *Clinical Obst and Gyn*, 61(2), 387-399,
https://www.ncbi.nlm.nih.gov/pmc/articles/PMC5915910/

[126] Hoffman, K. M., Trawalter, S., Axt, J. R.and Oliver, M. N. (2016) 'Racial bias in pain assessment and treatment recommendations, and false beliefs about biological differences between Blacks and Whites', *PNAS*, 113(16), 4296-4301,
https://www.pnas.org/content/113/16/4296

[127] Philby, C. (2018) 'Serena Williams and the realities of the 'maternal mortality crisis', *The Guardian*,
https://www.theguardian.com/lifeandstyle/shortcuts/2018/feb/21/serena-williams-maternal-mortality-crisis

[128] Schwartz, S. (2021) 'Map: Where Critical Race Theory Is Under Attack', *Education Week*,

https://www.edweek.org/policy-politics/map-where-critical-race-theory-is-under-attack/2021/06

[129] 'States That Have Banned Critical Race Theory 2022', *World Population Review*, https://worldpopulationreview.com/state-rankings/states-that-have-banned-critical-race-theory

[130] DeLuca, L. (2021) 'Black Inventor Garrett Morgan Saved Countless Lives with Gas Mask and Improved Traffic Lights', *Scientific American,* https://www.scientificamerican.com/article/Black-inventor-garrett-morgan-saved-countless-lives-with-gas-mask-and-improved-traffic-lights/

[131] Walton, A. (2021) 'How James E. West Co-Invented the Electret Microphone', *Afro Tech*, https://afrotech.com/how-james-e-west-co-invented-the-electret-microphone

[132] 'Mark Dean', Biography. https://www.biography.com/inventor/mark-dean#:~:text=Computer%20scientist%20and%20engineer%20Mark%20Dean%20helped%20develop%20a%20number,the%20company's%20original%20nine%20patents.

[133] Therrien, A. (2021) '120 things you probably didn't know were created by Black inventors', *Daily Hive.* https://dailyhive.com/seattle/inventions-by-Black-people

[134] 'School teacher workforce' (2023) Gov.uk.

https://www.ethnicity-facts-figures.service.gov.uk/workforce-and-business/workforce-diversity/school-teacher-workforce/latest#by-ethnicity

[135] Rhodes, D. (2017) 'Schools need 68,000 extra BME teachers to reflect population', *BBC News*, https://www.bbc.co.uk/news/uk-england-40568987

[136] Schaeffer, K. (2021) 'America's public school teachers are far less racially and ethnically diverse than their students', PEW Research Center, https://www.pewresearch.org/fact-tank/2021/12/10/americas-public-school-teachers-are-far-less-racially-and-ethnically-diverse-than-their-students/#:~:text=Since%20then%2C%20the%20number%20of,teachers%20has%20also%20grown%20steadily.

[137] IRR News Team (2020) 'How Black Working-Class Youth are Criminalised and Excluded in the English School System', *IRR*, https://irr.org.uk/article/beyond-the-pru-to-prison-pipeline/

[138] Dada, T. (2020) 'Pupils excluded from school might as well be given a prison sentence' — former Director-General', *TCS Network*, https://www.tcsnetwork.co.uk/young-people-excluded-from-school-might-as-well-be-given-a-prison-sentence-says-former-director-general/

[139] Glantz, A., and Martinez, E. (2018) 'Modern-day redlining: How banks block people of color from homeownership', *Chicago Tribune*,

https://www.chicagotribune.com/business/ct-biz-modern-day-redlining-20180215-story.html

[140] Smith, L., LaFond, K., Moehlman, L. (2018) 'Data analysis: 'Modern-day redlining' happening in Detroit and Lansing', *NPR,* https://www.michiganradio.org/news/2018-02-15/data-analysis-modern-day-redlining-happening-in-detroit-and-lansing

[141] Rivlin, G. (2016) 'White New Orleans Has Recovered from Hurricane Katrina. Black New Orleans Has Not', *Talk Poverty,* https://talkpoverty.org/2016/08/29/White-new-orleans-recovered-hurricane-katrina-Black-new-orleans-not/

[142] Doherty, C. (2015) 'Remembering Katrina: Wide racial divide over government's response', Pew Research Center, https://www.pewresearch.org/fact-tank/2015/08/27/remembering-katrina-wide-racial-divide-over-governments-response/

[143] Almasy, S., and Ly, L. (2017) 'Flint water crisis: Report says 'systemic racism' played role', *CNN,* https://edition.cnn.com/2017/02/18/politics/flint-water-report-systemic-racism/index.html

[144] Blum, W. (1996) 'The CIA, Contras, Gangs, and Crack', Institute for Policy Studies, https://ips-dc.org/the_cia_contras_gangs_and_crack/

[145] Wolfe-Rocca, U. 'COINTELPRO: Teaching the FBI's War on the Black Freedom Movement', Rethinking Schools,

https://rethinkingschools.org/articles/cointelpro-teaching-the-fbi-s-war-on-the-Black-freedom-movement/

[146] Sevilla, N. (2021) 'Food Apartheid: Racialized Access to Healthy Affordable Food', NRDC. https://www.nrdc.org/experts/nina-sevilla/food-apartheid-racialised-access-healthy-affordable-food

[147] 'African Genome Variation Project', Sanger Institute. https://www.sanger.ac.uk/collaboration/african-genome-variation-project/#:~:text=Our%20Project,-Genome%20Research%20Limited&text=As%20part%20of%20the%20African,African%20populations%20and%20ethnic%20groups.

[148] The Black Curriculum, https://theBlackcurriculum.com/

[149] 'Fair Housing Act', History.com. https://www.history.com/topics/Black-history/fair-housing-act

[150] HRC Staff (2019) '1964 Civil Rights Acts & The Equality Act', Human Rights Campaign, https://www.hrc.org/news/1964-civil-rights-acts-the-equality-act

[151] Shanay, M. (2018) 'T.I.'s 'Buy Back the Block' Venture Is Providing Affordable Housing', *The Jasmine Brand*, https://thejasminebrand.com/2018/10/13/t-i-s-buy-back-the-block-venture-is-providing-affordable-housing/

[152] Livingston, G. (2018) 'The Changing Profile of Unmarried Parents', Pew Research Center, https://www.pewresearch.org/social-trends/2018/04/25/the-changing-profile-of-unmarried-parents/#:~:text=Among%20solo%20parents%2C%2042%25%20are,cohabiting%20moms%20(30%25%20vs.

[153] 'Families and households', Gov.uk. https://www.ethnicity-facts-figures.service.gov.uk/uk-population-by-ethnicity/demographics/families-and-households/latest

[154] Brown, M. (2015) 'Fact check: United Kingdom finished paying off debts to slave-owning families in 2015', *USA Today*, https://eu.usatoday.com/story/news/factcheck/2020/06/30/fact-check-u-k-paid-off-debts-slave-owning-families-2015/3283908001/

[155] 'United States profile', Prison Policy Initiative. https://www.prisonpolicy.org/profiles/US.html#:~:text=With%20over%20two%20million%20people,1%25%20of%20our%20adult%20population.

[156] IBIS World (2023) 'Correctional Facilities Industry in the US — Market Research Report', IBIS World, https://www.ibisworld.com/united-states/market-research-reports/correctional-facilities-industry/

[157] Alexander, M. (2012) *The New Jim Crow Mass Incarceration in the Age of Colorblindness.*

[158] Beckett, K. (1997), (1999 Revised ed.) *Making Crime Pay: Law and Order in Contemporary American Politics*, Oxford: Oxford University Press; 'War on drugs', Wikipedia. https://en.wikipedia.org/wiki/War_on_drugs

[159] Lee, J. (2021) 'America has spent over a trillion dollars fighting the war on drugs. 50 years later, drug use in the U.S. is climbing again', *CNBC*, https://www.cnbc.com/2021/06/17/the-us-has-spent-over-a-trillion-dollars-fighting-war-on-drugs.html

[160] The White House. (2021) 'Biden-Harris Administration Calls for Historic Levels of Funding to Prevent and Treat Addiction and Overdose', White house.Gov. https://www.Whitehouse.gov/ondcp/briefing-room/2021/05/28/biden-harris-administration-calls-for-historic-levels-of-funding-to-prevent-and-treat-addiction-and-overdose/

[161] 'Terry v. Ohio, 392 U.S. 1' (1968) US Supreme Court, https://supreme.justia.com/cases/federal/us/392/1/

[162] 'Stop and search' (2022) Gov.uk. https://www.ethnicity-facts-figures.service.gov.uk/crime-justice-and-the-law/policing/stop-and-search/latest

[163] Ruhl, C. (2023) 'The Broken Windows Theory', Simply Psychology, https://www.simplypsychology.org/broken-windows-theory.html

[164] 'H.R.3355 — Violent Crime Control and Law Enforcement Act of 1994', Congress.gov.
https://www.congress.gov/bill/103rd-congress/house-bill/3355

[165] Lussenhop, J. (2016) 'Clinton crime bill: Why is it so controversial?' *BBC News*,
https://www.bbc.co.uk/news/world-us-canada-36020717

[166] The Sentencing Project (2018) 'Report to the United Nations on Racial Disparities in the U.S. Criminal Justice System', Sentencing Project.org,
https://www.sentencingproject.org/publications/un-report-on-racial-disparities/

[167] 'Racial Disparities on the War on Drugs', Human Rights Watch,
https://www.hrw.org/legacy/campaigns/drugs/war/key-facts.htm

[168] Vagins, D. J., and McCurdy, J. (2006) 'Cracks in the System. Twenty Years of the Unjust Federal Crack Cocaine Law', ACLU.org,
https://www.aclu.org/sites/default/files/pdfs/drugpolicy/cracksinsystem_20061025.pdf

[169] 'The Crisis of the Young African American Male and the Criminal Justice System', Sentencing Project.org,
https://www.sentencingproject.org/wp-content/uploads/2016/01/Crisis-of-the-Young-African-American-Male-and-the-Criminal-Justice-System.pdf

[170] Vagins, D. J., and McCurdy, J. (2006) 'Cracks in the System. Twenty Years of the Unjust Federal Crack Cocaine Law', ACLU.org, https://www.aclu.org/sites/default/files/pdfs/drugpolicy/cracksinsystem_20061025.pdf

[171] Nellis, A. (2021) 'The Color of Justice: Racial and Ethnic Disparity in State Prisons', The Sentencing Project, https://www.sentencingproject.org/publications/color-of-justice-racial-and-ethnic-disparity-in-state-prisons/

[172] Bowen, P. (2019) 'Building Trust: How our courts can improve the criminal court experience for Black, Asian, and Minority Ethnic defendants', Centre for Justice Innovation, https://justiceinnovation.org/sites/default/files/media/documents/2019-03/building-trust.pdf

[173] 'Police and Criminal Evidence Act 1984 (PACE) — Code A' (2014) Home Office, https://assets.publishing.service.gov.uk/government/uploads/system/uploads/attachment_data/file/384122/PaceCodeAWeb.pdf

[174] Dodd, V. (2020) 'Black people nine times more likely to face stop and search than White people', *The Guardian*, https://www.theguardian.com/uk-news/2020/oct/27/Black-people-nine-times-more-likely-to-face-stop-and-search-than-White-people

[175] Grierson, J. (2020) 'Met carried out 22,000 searches on young Black men during lockdown', *The Guardian*, https://www.theguardian.com/law/2020/jul/08/one-in-10-of-londons-young-Black-males-stopped-by-police-in-may

[176] 'Arrests' (2022) Gov.uk. https://www.ethnicity-facts-figures.service.gov.uk/crime-justice-and-the-law/policing/number-of-arrests/latest

[177] 'Stop and search in England and Wales', Full Fact. https://fullfact.org/crime/stop-and-search-england-and-wales/#:~:text=Only%209%25%20of%20stops%20and,arrest%20in%20the%20same%20year.

[178] BBC News (2015) 'UK to build £25m Jamaican prison', *BBC News*, https://www.bbc.co.uk/news/uk-34398014

[179] Gentleman, A. (2020) 'Windrush scandal: only 60 victims given compensation so far', *The Guardian*, https://www.theguardian.com/uk-news/2020/may/28/windrush-scandal-only-60-victims-given-compensation-so-far

[180] The Guardian team (2018) 'The Guardian view on the Windrush generation: the scandal isn't over', *The Guardian*, https://www.theguardian.com/commentisfree/2018/oct/17/the-guardian-view-on-the-windrush-generation-the-scandal-isnt-over

[181] Afzal, N. (2020) 'Black people dying in police custody should surprise no one', *The Guardian,* https://www.theguardian.com/uk-news/2020/jun/11/Black-deaths-in-police-custody-the-tip-of-an-iceberg-of-racist-treatment

[182] Migiro, G. (2018) 'Where Is the African Diaspora?' World Atlas, https://www.worldatlas.com/articles/where-is-the-african-Diaspora.html

[183] Ramos, P.C., and Völker, S. (2020) 'Police Violence Against Black People Is on the Rise in Brazil', *GIGA*, 5, https://www.giga-hamburg.de/en/publications/giga-focus/police-violence-against-Black-people-is-on-the-rise-in-brazil

[184] 'Operation Hotton Learning report', PoliceConduct.gov.uk. https://www.policeconduct.gov.uk/sites/default/files/Operation%20Hotton%20Learning%20report%20-%20January%202022.pdf

[185] 'Voting Rights Act of 1965', History.com. https://www.history.com/topics/Black-history/voting-rights-act#:~:text=The%20Voting%20Rights%20Act%20of,Amendment%20to%20the%20U.S.%20Constitution.

[186] Sullivan, A. (2019) 'Southern U.S. states have closed 1,200 polling places in recent years: rights group', *Reuters*, https://www.reuters.com/article/us-usa-election-locations-idUSKCN1VV09J

[187] Ax, J. (2022) 'Texas rejects hundreds of mail ballot applications under new voting limits', *Reuters,* https://www.reuters.com/world/us/texas-rejects-hundreds-mail-ballot-applications-under-new-voting-limits-2022-01-18/

[188] Killough, A., and Kelly, C. (2020) 'Texas Supreme Court sides with governor on rule requiring one ballot drop box per county', *CNN*, https://edition.cnn.com/2020/10/27/politics/texas-supreme-court-drop-boxes/index.html

[189] Levine, S. (2020) 'US supreme court deals setback to Republicans over mail-in voting in key states', *The Guardian*, https://www.theguardian.com/us-news/2020/oct/28/pennsylvania-elections-ballot-extension-supreme-court

[190] 'Voters struggling with witness rules in early voting', *ABC News*. https://abcnews.go.com/Health/wireStory/witness-mandate-vex-mail-voters-key-states-73239572

[191] Pennsylvania's naked ballot problem, explained, *Vox*. https://www.vox.com/21452393/naked-ballots-pennsylvania-secrecy-envelope

[192] Levine, S. (2020) 'More than 10-hour wait and long lines as early voting starts in Georgia', *The Guardian*, https://www.theguardian.com/us-news/2020/oct/13/more-than-10-hour-wait-and-long-lines-as-early-voting-starts-in-georgia

[193] Levinson-King, R. (2020) 'US election 2020: Why it can be hard to vote in the US', *BBC News*, https://www.bbc.co.uk/news/election-us-2020-54240651

[194] Ensure Every American Can Vote (2021) 'Voting Laws Roundup: December 2021', https://www.brennancenter.org/our-work/research-reports/voting-laws-roundup-december-2021

[195] Department for Education (2011) 'Plans to end the Education Maintenance Allowance (EMA) programme'. Gov.uk, https://www.gov.uk/government/news/plans-to-end-the-education-maintenance-allowance-ema-programme

[196] Williams, M. (2017) 'How students have been misled and lied to for 20 years', *Channel 4 News*, https://www.channel4.com/news/factcheck/factcheck-how-students-have-been-misled-and-lied-to-for-20-years

[197] BBC News (2020) 'China McDonald's apologises for Guangzhou ban on Black people', *BBC News*, https://www.bbc.co.uk/news/world-asia-china-52274326

[198] Fröhlich, S. (2022) 'Thousands of African students are stuck in Ukraine', DW.com. https://www.dw.com/en/thousands-of-african-students-are-stuck-in-ukraine/a-60902104

[199] Debuysere, L. (2020) 'Why the EU should take the global lead in cancelling Africa's debt', *CEPS*. https://www.ceps.eu/why-the-eu-should-take-the-global-lead-in-cancelling-africas-debt/

[200] Omotola, J. S. and Saliu, H. (2009) 'Foreign aid, debt relief and Africa's development: problems and prospects', *South African Journal of International Affairs*, 16(1), 87-102.

[201] Facing History & Ourselves. (2017) 'Inventing Black and White', https://www.facinghistory.org/holocaust-and-human-behavior/chapter-2/inventing-Black-and-White

[202] Wright, B. C. T. (2023) 'Violent White Folks Who Were Taken into Custody With Loving Care By Police', *NewsOne*, https://newsone.com/playlist/White-arrested-with-by-police/

[203] 'The Bristol Bus Boycott of 1963', Black History Month, https://www.Blackhistorymonth.org.uk/article/section/bhm-heroes/the-bristol-bus-boycott-of-1963/

[204] 'The Birmingham Campaign', *PBS*, http://www.pbs.org/Black-culture/explore/civil-rights-movement-birmingham-campaign/

[205] Wamsley, L., and Allyn, B. (2019) 'Neo-Nazi Who Killed Charlottesville Protester Is Sentenced to Life In Prison', *NPR*, https://www.npr.org/2019/06/28/736915323/neo-nazi-who-killed-charlottesville-protester-is-sentenced-to-life-in-prison

[206] BBC News (2023) 'Capitol riots timeline: What happened on 6 January 2021?' *BBC News*, https://www.bbc.co.uk/news/world-us-canada-56004916

[207] Jewkes, Y. and Gooch, K. (2019) How lessons in Scandinavian design could help prisons with rehabilitation, *The Conversation*, https://theconversation.com/how-lessons-in-scandinavian-design-could-help-prisons-with-rehabilitation-106554

[208] Cox, C. (2020) 'The claim: Joe Biden referred to Black people as 'super predators' during the passage of the 1994 crime bill', *USA Today News*, https://eu.usatoday.com/story/news/factcheck/2020/10/24/fact-check-hillary-clinton-called-some-criminals-super-predators/6021383002/

[209] Earp, C. (2020) 'X Factor star Misha B accuses the show of creating bullying storyline that left her suicidal', *Digital Spy*, https://www.digitalspy.com/tv/reality-tv/a32863826/x-factor-misha-b-bully-claims/

[210] Berman, R. (2018) 'Was Elvis Presley a cultural appropriator of Black music?' *Big Think*, https://bigthink.com/culture-religion/would-elvis-be-considered-a-cultural-appropriator-today/

[211] Hinton, R. (2015) Dylann Roof 'loner' rhetoric excuses the inexcusable, *The DePaulia*, https://depauliaonline.com/12837/opinions/dylann-roof-loner-ill-inexcusable/

[212] Lopez, G. (2014) 'Police thought 12-year-old Tamir Rice was 20 when they shot him. This isn't uncommon', *Vox*, https://www.vox.com/2014/11/26/7297265/tamir-rice-age-police

[213] Fung, K. (2012) Geraldo Rivera: Trayvon Martin's 'Hoodie Is As Much Responsible For [His] Death As George Zimmerman' (VIDEO), *The Huffington Post*, https://www.huffingtonpost.co.uk/entry/geraldo-rivera-trayvon-martin-hoodie_n_1375080

[214] The Daily Mail (2018) 'Young Manchester City footballer, 20, on £25,000 a week splashes out on mansion on market for £2.25million despite having never started a Premier League match', *The Daily Mail*, https://www.dailymail.co.uk/news/article-5253633/Man-City-footballer-20-25k-week-buys-market-2-25m-home.html

[215] Sterling, R. (2018) 'Raheem Sterling: Newspapers help 'fuel racism' with portrayals of young Black players', *ITV*, https://www.itv.com/news/2018-12-09/raheem-sterling-police-investigate-alleged-racist-abuse-aimed-at-manchester-city-star

[216] Mohdin, A. (2017) 'The media ends up racializing poverty by presenting a distorted image of Black families', Quartz, https://qz.com/1158041/study-media-portrayal-of-Black-families-versus-White-families-in-the-us/

[217] Desmond-Harris, J., 'NYC media coverage of Black suspects is way out of proportion with Black arrest rates', *Vox*,

https://www.vox.com/2015/3/26/8296091/media-bias-race-crime

[218] NL Team. (2022) 'Europeans with blue eyes, blonde hair being killed': Media coverage of Ukraine criticised for racism', *News Laundry*. https://www.newslaundry.com/2022/02/28/europeans-with-blue-eyes-blonde-hair-being-killed-media-coverage-of-ukraine-criticised-for-racism

[219] Finley, T. (2018) 'Sterling K. Brown Is the First Black Man to Win Golden Globe for Best Actor in Drama', *HuffPost*. https://www.huffingtonpost.co.uk/entry/sterling-k-brown-golden-globe-best-actor_n_5a52addbe4b003133ec915ef#:~:text=Sterling%20K.-,Brown%20Is%20The%20First%20Black%20Man%20To%20Win%20Golden%20Globe,played%20by%20a%20Black%20man.%22

[220] Brinkhurst-Cuff, C. (2017) 'Is Love Racist? The TV show laying our biases bare', *The Guardian*, https://www.theguardian.com/tv-and-radio/2017/jul/17/is-love-racist-the-tv-show-laying-our-biases-bare

[221] Jackie Robinson Quotes, https://jackierobinson.com/quotes/

[222] Aarons, E. (2019) 'England Euro 2020 qualifier in Sofia halted twice over racist abuse', *The Guardian*, https://www.theguardian.com/football/2019/oct/14/england-euro-2020-qualifier-in-sofia-halted-twice-over-racist-abuse

[223] BBC Sport (2021) 'Racist abuse of England players Marcus Rashford, Jadon Sancho & Bukayo Saka ''unforgivable''', *BBC Sport,*
https://www.bbc.co.uk/sport/football/57800431

[224] BBC News (2020) 'Raheem Sterling: Man City fans banned for racist abuse', *BBC News,*
https://www.bbc.co.uk/news/uk-england-manchester-51066328

[225] Chelsea Core Desk (2018) 'Chelsea Fan Hurls Racist Abuse at Raheem Sterling', *Chelsea Core,*
https://chelseacore.com/chelsea-fan-racist-abuse-raheem-sterling/

[226] Čizmić, A. (2020) 'Why Italian football remains racist', *New Frame,*
https://www.newframe.com/why-italian-football-remains-racist/

[227] HISTORY.COM Editors (2020) 'Negro League Baseball', History.com.
https://www.history.com/topics/sports/negro-league-baseball

[228] Reid, J., and McManus, J. (2017) 'The NFL's racial divide', *The Undefeated,*
https://theundefeated.com/features/the-nfls-racial-divide/

[229] Coleman, C. A., and Scott, J. (2018) 'Sports are not Colorblind: The Role of Race and Segregation in NFL Positions', *Journal of Emerging Investigators,*

https://www.theneighborhoodacademy.org/editoruploads/files/sportscolorblind_final.pdf

[230] Mayer, S. (2010) *Gods of the Gridiron: The Racial Characterisation of Quarterbacks in Sports Illustrated*, Saint Mary's College Undergraduate Dissertation, https://www.saintmarys.edu/files/sarah%20mayer.pdf

[231] Prior, I. (2004) 'TV pundit Ron Atkinson sacked for racist remark', *The Guardian*, https://www.theguardian.com/media/2004/apr/22/football.raceintheuk

[232] Spears, M. (2021) 'Jaylen Brown on why it's important for the Celtics and NBA to hire African American head coaches', *The Undefeated*, https://theundefeated.com/features/jaylen-brown-on-why-its-important-for-celtics-and-nba-to-hire-african-american-head-coaches/

[233] Cunningham, G. B. (2022) 'When the Rooney Rule doesn't work: the NFL's terrible track record on diversity', *Fast Company*, https://www.fastcompany.com/90716789/when-the-rooney-rule-doesnt-work-the-nfls-terrible-track-record-on-diversity

[234] Olley, J. (2021) 'Football still discriminates against Black managers, but it won't put me off trying — Euell', *ESPN*, https://www.espn.co.uk/football/blog-espn-fc-united/story/4507003/football-still-discriminates-against-Black-managers-but-it-wont-put-me-off-trying-euell

[235] Ramaswamy, S.V. (2022) 'NFL Rooney Rule and business: Experts say the hiring practice 'requires vigilance'', *USA Today Money*,
https://eu.usatoday.com/story/money/2022/02/02/rooney-rule-nfl-hiring-interview/6638223001/

[236] 'Rooney Rule', *Wikipedia*
https://en.wikipedia.org/wiki/Rooney_Rule

[237] WCC Sports. (2020) 'Russell Rule Diversity Hiring Commitment',
https://wccsports.com/news/2020/8/2/general-russell-rule-diversity-hiring-commitment.aspx

[238] 'Football Leadership Diversity Codes', The FA,
https://www.thefa.com/football-rules-governance/inclusion-and-anti-discrimination/football-leadership-diversity-code

[239] Frantz Fanon, *The Wretched of the Earth*.

[240] The National Council of Mental Well Being. (2019) 'Stigma Regarding Mental Illness among People of Color', The National Council of Mental Well Being,
https://www.thenationalcouncil.org/BH365/2019/07/08/stigma-regarding-mental-illness-among-people-of-color/

[241] 'Black, Asian and minority ethnic (BAME) communities', MentalHealth.org,
https://www.mentalhealth.org.uk/a-to-z/b/Black-asian-and-minority-ethnic-bame-communities

[242] National Alliance to End Homelessness. (2023) 'Homelessness and Racial Disparities', https://endhomelessness.org/homelessness-in-america/what-causes-homelessness/inequality/

[243] 'Mental and Behavioral Health — African Americans', Minority Health, https://minorityhealth.hhs.gov/omh/browse.aspx?lvl=4&lvlid=24

[244] 'Inmate Race', Federal Bureau of Prisons, https://www.bop.gov/about/statistics/statistics_inmate_race.jsp

[245] 'Jail can be scary'…mental health in prison', Mental Health.org, https://www.mentalhealth.org.uk/blog/jail-can-be-scary-mental-health-prison#:~:text=The%20Institute%20of%20Psychiatry%20estimated,and%20serious%20mental%20health%20problems

[246] Bignall, T., Jeraj, S., Helsby, E. and Butt, J. (2022) *Racial disparities in mental health: Literature and evidence review*, https://raceequalityfoundation.org.uk/wp-content/uploads/2022/10/mental-health-report-v5-2.pdf

[247] MIND (2019) 'Discrimination in mental health services', Mind.org. https://www.mind.org.uk/news-campaigns/legal-news/legal-newsletter-june-2019/discrimination-in-mental-health-services/

[248] NatCen Social Research and the Department of Health Sciences, University of Leicester. (2014) *Mental Health and Wellbeing in England*, NHS Digital, https://assets.publishing.service.gov.uk/government/uploads/system/uploads/attachment_data/file/556596/apms-2014-full-rpt.pdf

[249] Race Equality Foundation. (2018) 'African and Caribbean men and mental health', https://raceequalityfoundation.org.uk/wp-content/uploads/2018/03/health-brief5.pdf

[250] Khan, L., Saini, G., Augustine, A. Palmer, K., Johnson M., and Donald, R. (2017) *Against the odds: Evaluation of the Mind Birmingham Up My Street programme*, Centre for Mental Health. https://www.mind.org.uk/media-a/4300/ums-report.pdf

[251] NHS Digital. (2014) *Adult Psychiatric Morbidity Survey: Survey of Mental Health and Wellbeing, England*, https://digital.nhs.uk/data-and-information/publications/statistical/adult-psychiatric-morbidity-survey/adult-psychiatric-morbidity-survey-survey-of-mental-health-and-wellbeing-england-2014

[252] Detentions under the Mental Health Act, Gov.uk. https://www.ethnicity-facts-figures.service.gov.uk/health/mental-health/detentions-under-the-mental-health-act/latest

[253] Gajwani, R., Parsons, H., Birchwood, M., Singh, S. (2016) 'Ethnicity and detention: are Black and minority ethnic (BME)

groups disproportionately detained under the Mental Health Act 2007?', *Soc Psychiatry Psychiatr Epidemiol*, 51(5), 703-11, https://pubmed.ncbi.nlm.nih.gov/26886264/

[254] 'Black/African American, National Alliance on Mental Illness', https://nami.org/Your-Journey/Identity-and-Cultural-Dimensions/Black-African-American

[255] Snowden, L. R., Catalano, R., and Shumway, M. (2009) 'Disproportionate Use of Psychiatric Emergency Services by African Americans', *Psychiatry Services*, 60(12), 1664-1671 https://ps.psychiatryonline.org/doi/10.1176/ps.2009.60.12.1664

[256] Xu, K., Nosek, B., and Greenwald A. G. (2014) 'Psychology data from the Race Implicit Association Test on the Project Implicit Demo website', *Journal of Open Psychology Data*, 2(1), https://openpsychologydata.metajnl.com/articles/10.5334/jopd.ac/

[257] Brown, G., Marshall, M., Bower, P., Woodham, A., and Waheed, W. (2014) 'Barriers to recruiting ethnic minorities to mental health research: a systematic review', *International Journal of Methods in Psychiatry Research*, 23(1): 36-48, https://www.ncbi.nlm.nih.gov/pmc/articles/PMC6878438/

[258] King, C. (2019) 'Race, mental health, and the research gap', *The Lancet Psychiatry*, 6(5), 367-368. https://www.thelancet.com/journals/lanpsy/article/PIIS2215-0366(19)30091-4/fulltext

[259] Black Minds Matter, https://www.Blackmindsmatteruk.com/

[260] Black, African and Asian Therapist Network, https://www.baatn.org.uk/

[261] BEAM Black Emotional and Mental Health, https://beam.community/about/#:~:text=Our%20Mission,advocacy%2C%20and%20the%20creative%20arts.

[262] Therapy for Black Girls, https://therapyforBlackgirls.com/

[263] McKinsey & Company. (2021) *Psychological safety and the critical role of leadership development*, McKinsey & Company. https://www.mckinsey.com/business-functions/people-and-organisational-performance/our-insights/psychological-safety-and-the-critical-role-of-leadership-development

[264] The CROWN Act. https://www.thecrownact.com/

[265] 'Nelson Mandela speech, Madison Park High School, Boston, June 23, 1990.' (ed.) Radcliffe, S., *Oxford Essential Quotations*, https://www.oxfordreference.com/view/10.1093/acref/9780191843730.001.0001/q-oro-ed5-00007046

[266] Sonmez, F. (2022) 'House passes anti-lynching bill that Rep. Bobby Rush says is decades overdue', *The Washington Post*.

https://www.washingtonpost.com/politics/2022/02/28/house-expected-pass-antilynching-bill-two-years-after-sen-rand-paul-blocked-unanimous-passage/

Milton Keynes UK
Ingram Content Group UK Ltd.
UKHW022217181123
432823UK00011B/255

9 781398 482241